D0728273

The Florence Prescription

From Accountability to Ownership

The Next Frontier for Patient Satisfaction,
Workplace Productivity, and Employee Loyalty

By Joe Tye
(with Dick Schwab)

Foreword by Charles S. Lauer
Former Executive Publisher of *Modern Healthcare* and author of *Decency*

The Florence Prescription

Quantity discounts are available: Call the Values Coach Office at 800-644-3889.

ISBN#: 978-1-887511-27-8

Cover: Detail from *Florence Nightingale Receiving the Wounded at Scutari* — 1856 — The Mission of Mercy by Jerry Barrett, 1824-1906. Oil on canvas

Cover and Interior Layout Design/Production: Studio 6 Sense · www.6sense.net

Dedication

For Sally & Katherine, our ladies with the lamp

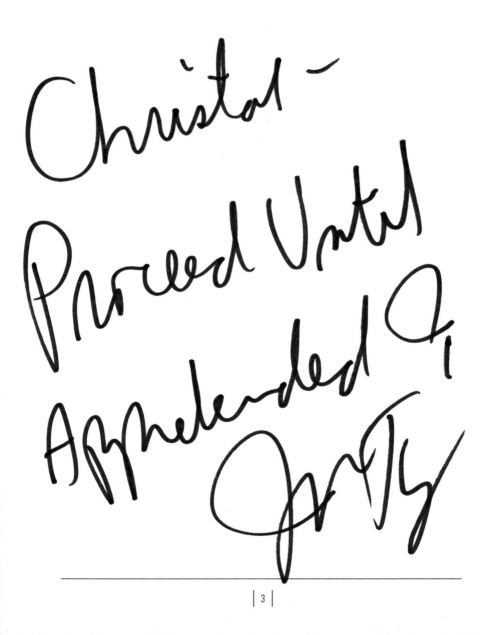

Christal —
Proceed Until
Apprehended

Advance Praise

for the *Florence Prescription*

"Required reading for any healthcare leader that wants to set their organization apart from all others. Joe Tye and Dick Schwab bring to life the wisdom of Florence Nightingale. In this fictional story they compel leaders to restore core values like compassion, respect, dignity and ownership as the only way to truly differentiate. The message from Nightingale is loud and clear... 'we must do better than this' and it means more today than ever before."

M. Bridget Duffy, M.D., Chief Experience Officer, Cleveland Clinic Foundation

---

"The Florence Prescription contains that unbeatable formula of timeless and timely wisdom packaged in a thoroughly entertaining story. In this story, Carol Jean Hawtrey reminds us that in these unpredictable times, organizations need leadership in every corner, not just in the corner office. Everyone – and I mean everyone – who works in a hospital can benefit from reading this book. Every healthcare leader should be striving to build a culture of ownership in his or her organization, and this book is the clearest and most helpful guide I've seen for achieving that cultural transformation."

David G. Altman, Ph.D., Executive Vice President for Research, Innovation & Product Development, Center for Creative Leadership

---

"The Florence Prescription is a delightful read because of the compelling case it makes for deploying the enduring and profound strategies 'the first professional hospital administrator – Florence Nightingale' made in her work almost 100 years ago. Her masterful blend of compassion, courage and discipline changed the lives of countless soldiers and can be an inspiration for healthcare leaders today. Part fiction, part reality, The Florence Prescription is fun to read and then pass on to all your colleagues."

Todd Linden, President and CEO, Grinnell Regional Medical Center

---

"*The Florence Prescription* speaks to the heart of changes that must occur in hospitals. In prescribing the eight essential characteristics of a culture of owner-ship, Florence doesn't let anyone off the hook. From executive leadership to frontline workers, everyone must play a part – and this book shows the way."

David Corbin, author of *Illuminate: Breakthrough Results Using The Positive Power of Negative Thinking* and *Psyched On Service*

The Florence Prescription
From Accountability to Ownership

"Instilling patient-centered care is not just about changing policies and practices; it is about changing culture, which is never easily done. For staff to be empathetic to patients, the hospital must also have an empathetic culture for staff... To achieve a culture that is patient-centered and supportive of staff, hospital leadership and staff must share common beliefs and values. Coming to these common beliefs and values may be the hardest part of achieving cultural change."

Health Care at the Crossroads: Guiding Principles for the Development of the Hospital of the Future, a white paper by The Joint Commission

---

"One does not have to look far today to see that many of Florence Nightingale's greatest concerns remain ours too. In the closing months of 2007, news stories continually surfaced, revealing deep-seated problems in health care she would certainly have recognized, and which would have alarmed and exercised her."

Mark Bostridge: *Florence Nightingale: The Making of an Icon*

"Florence Nightingale became an incarnation of the values of the British people. She personified courage, selflessness, determination, industry, initiative, tenderness, compassion. By a unique combination of events, Florence Nightingale had attained a unique power."

Gillian Gill: *Nightingales: The Extraordinary Upbringing and Curious Life of Miss Florence Nightingale*

"Nightingale's enduring legacy is socially relevant because the profession of nursing shows signs of losing its soul; it is in crisis."

Barbara Montgomery Dossey et al: *Florence Nightingale Today: Healing, Leadership, Global Action*

Other books by Joe Tye

Fiction

The Healing Tree: A Poet, A Mermaid, and A Miracle

Never Fear, Never Quit: A Story of Courage and Perseverance

Your Dreams Are Too Small

The Farmer

Nonfiction

The Twelve Core Action Values

Leadership Lessons: What You Can Learn from J.R.R. Tolkien's Classic Works

Take the Stairs (with Roger Looyenga)

Personal Best: 1001 Great Ideas for Achieving Success in Your Career

Staying on Top When the World's Upside Down

Winning the War with Yourself Field Manual (workbook)

Eight Essential Characteristics of a Culture of Ownership

Commitment

Engagement

Passion

Initiative

Stewardship

Belonging

Fellowship

Pride

Contents

Foreword by Charles S. Lauer

The Florence Prescription is a new inspirational book written by Joe Tye and Dick Schwab of Values Coach Inc. The book reminds us of the abiding and profound influence of one of healthcare's greatest heroes: Florence Nightingale. Unless you happen to be a nurse, Florence Nightingale is a person whose name doesn't always come up in conversations about the healthcare business. And yet, she embodies the compassion, caring and enduring commitment that are so vital to healthcare's identify as a profession, discipline, industry and vocational calling.

Educated, well-to-do, and well connected, Ms. Nightingale was a British woman who was named after the city of her birth: Florence, Italy. During the Crimean War of the 1850s, Ms. Nightingale earned her moniker: "The Lady with the Lamp." In the face of horrific wartime conditions, she ministered to wounded and dying soldiers, leaving such a "heartprint" that she was immortalized in a poem by poet Henry Wadsworth Longfellow:

> *Lo! in that hour of misery*
> *A lady with a lamp I see*
> *Pass through the glimmering gloom,*
> *And flit from room to room.*

The rest, of course, is history. The Nightingale School of Nursing, the first educational training program for nurses, was founded in Great Britain in 1860 and continues to this day at the University of Southampton. International Nurses Day is celebrated each year in Ms. Nightingale's honor and she continues to serve as an inspiration to millions of healthcare professionals who realize the healthcare must reach beyond the bottom line to truly achieve greatness. Healthcare may be a business. But as Karl Bays, the CEO of American Hospital

Supply once told me, "Healthcare is a business of caring for patients and families."

In making Florence Nightingale the conscience, guide and sage of their book, Joe Tye and Dick Schwab remind us that no matter now significant our clinical, technological and business breakthroughs, healthcare is most likely to realize its mission, vision and values through a single ingredient: people. Healthcare's identity is rooted in the patients and families it serves, but it's also anchored in the people – from techs and physicians, to dieticians and nurses – who serve and minister to the needs of patients and families.

Think about it for a minute. What would healthcare be without men of courage like Gail Warden, C. Everett Koop, Paul Elwood or Robert Wood Johnson. How much less would healthcare have accomplished were it not for women like Clara Barton, Mother Elizabeth Ann Seton, or Ann Ramsey Somers?

The Florence Prescription reminds of the importance of healthcare heroes – as sources of intelligence and inspiration, and as the conscience for everything we say, do and feel. Such individuals, including Florence Nightingale, remind us that although we face a crisis in healthcare, that crisis is as much internal as it is external. As we struggle to come to grips with the challenges of technology, payment, and clinical care, we must also have the courage to look in the mirror and find what Abraham Lincoln called "the better angels of our nature."

Following are just some of the lessons learned that I hope you'll experience by reading *The Florence Prescription*:

- Remember that healthcare isn't just a business; it's a mission. Just as important, serving as a caregiver or healthcare executive is far more than a job; it's a calling and lifetime commitment.

- Develop a Lexus mindset. Consider your personal and professional life, as well as the centuries old saga of health and medicine, as "the relentless pursuit of perfection." None of our problems will be solved in a year or even 10 years. And yet, each day we can make significant but meaningful incremental changes and propel healthcare forward.

- Look to the healthcare heroes who may be standing over your shoulder. They can help you and your colleagues rekindle the same sense of mission and service that empowered Florence Nightingale to confront and overcome conditions far worse than any we face today.

- Reflect on the three essential questions of life: Mission: Why are we here? Vision: Where are we headed? Values: What do we believe in? What are the standards and criteria by which we will make decisions? Getting a handle on your values – whether they happen to include service, perseverance, candor or fun – will shape your choices and decisions and transform your life.

- Reach new altitudes with the right attitudes. Healthcare professionals bring knowledge, skill and experience to their jobs. But few credentials, awards and achievements can compensate for a dreary or rude attitude toward co-workers and patients. Patients and providers deserve co-workers who are positive, optimistic, hopeful and confident in the future. Let's leave gossip, complaining and ridicule where it belongs – at the back door.

- Invest in people – a healthcare organization's greatest asset. Inspire people to think and act as innovators, entrepreneurs and owners. As Carol Jean Hawtrey says in *The Florence Prescription*, relate to people as if they are partners in the enterprise and not just renting a spot on the organizational chart.

- Foster partnership and collaboration. Achieving healthcare's vision of authentic patient-centered care requires that we function as partners and team-members, not divas, drama queens or superstars. Humility, unconditional positive regard and a willingness to share in both victory and defeat will go a long way in helping healthcare to achieve its goals.

In my 30 years as publisher of *Modern Healthcare*, I gradually came to realize what really matters in this, America's most exciting industry.

Joint ventures, mergers and acquisitions and regulatory changes tend to come and go. What remains, however, is the courage, dignity and good will of patients and families and the people who serve them. In my new and emerging role as a healthcare speaker and consultant, I've come to another realization: People are hungry to rediscover the heart of healthcare. *The Florence Prescription* goes a long way in helping us on that journey of rediscovery.

Best wishes,
Charles S. Lauer

Mr. Lauer can be contacted at chuckspeaking@aol.com or at 312-816-3364. Learn more about his speaking and consulting services at www.chucklauer.com and www.chucklauer.net.

The *Florence Prescription* is a fictional story about an imagined medical center populated by made-up characters, but the message is genuine and it is urgent. The health care crisis of the early 21st century isn't just about financing and access – it is also a crisis of culture, and of confidence. It is doubtful that any healthcare leader ever faced a crisis more serious than the disaster zone that was the Scutari Barrack Hospital when Florence Nightingale arrived in 1854 to care for British casualties of the Crimean War. Yet over the next two years she transformed the entire operation, creating what was in effect a blueprint for the hospital as we know it today. In the following years, Nightingale and her intrepid band of healthcare pioneers brought about sweeping changes in hospital design, nursing education, and public health.

But this book is not about what Florence Nightingale did (we've included a bibliography for learning more about that). Rather, we ask this question: What would Florence Nightingale tell us to do for our hospitals were she to return today. We believe she would tell us that Job #1 is to re-spark the spirit of purpose and mission that once did, and always should, inspire people who have committed their professional lives to caring for others. We believe she would say that while it is important to hold people accountable for their performance and their outcomes, that's not enough. In today's complex and dynamic world, we must go beyond mere accountability and foster a culture of ownership where people hold themselves accountable because they have personal buy-in to the values and mission of their hospitals.

The Florence Prescription is a story that we hope will both inform and inspire anyone who works in healthcare today. The eight essential characteristics that we describe for a culture of ownership – commitment, engagement, passion, initiative, stewardship, belonging, fellowship and pride – also happen to be essential ingredients for personal success and happiness. Ultimately, *The Florence Prescription* is more than a program or a prescription. It is a way of life.

We chose the fictional format for two reasons. First, as Christopher Tolkien has noted, fictional characters can be more real than real people because they can be distilled to the essence of their being, and through the eyes of the author the reader can see into their souls. Second, fiction allows for time compression. In fiction, we can transform the culture of Memorial Medical Center in the time it takes a reader to fly from Chicago to Los Angeles. In real life, we all know that the process is much messier, more arduous, and takes a whole lot longer. And that while fictional stories eventually reach "The End," in real life the work is never really done.

It's been said that the truth is more important than the facts. This story, while fictional, is also true. It draws from our own experiences as senior executives in big organizations (Joe as chief operating officer of a large community teaching hospital and Dick as a corporate CEO and chair of a hospital board), and from our work at Values Coach helping hospitals promote values-based leadership and cultural transformation. We are convinced that before you can truly transform the culture of an organization, you must invest in helping people transform the quality of their lives, and that you do that by helping them connect the work they do with their most deeply-held values. Making that connection is the first step toward fostering a culture of ownership.

In these challenging times, hospitals and other healthcare organizations need every possible hand on the oars. Fostering a culture of ownership isn't just about creating a nice environment in which to work and receive care, though that it is. A culture of ownership is the *sine qua non* for recruiting and retaining great people, ensuring optimal productivity and safe patient-centered care, and meeting the increasingly tough demands being placed on our industry by society at large. Today's hospitals can't survive, much less thrive, with hired hands on the job – they need people who think like partners, people who own their work rather than just renting a spot on the organization chart. They need *The Florence Prescription.*

Joe Tye and Dick Schwab
Solon, Iowa
March, 2009

December, 1854

The hour was half past midnight. The Lady with the Lamp made her way slowly through the corridors filled with wounded, sick and dying soldiers, clear-headed and broken-hearted. The men were jammed together along the floors like too many plants packed into a row of beans, their only mattress the fetid and bloodied straw that was spread across the floors. The lucky ones had a blanket to themselves. "We can do better than this," Florence Nightingale whispered into the foul air of the old Turkish army barracks building that had, almost as an afterthought, been converted into a hospital for British casualties of the war against Russia in the far-off Crimean Peninsula. "We must do better than this."

Nightingale knelt beside a young soldier who was crying for his mother. He would, she knew, die during the night watch. "They always cry for their mothers," she thought as she pulled the last orange from her apron pocket. She peeled away a slice and, gently lifting the young man's head, squeezed the juice into his mouth. His eyes flickered open. "Thank you." Nightingale saw, rather than heard, his last words, words she had so often seen on the lips of dying men so grateful for the most trivial of kindnesses. *We must do better than this.* The young man drifted back into his final sleep. As she so often did for dying soldiers, Nightingale massaged his feet. "Soldiers live on their feet," Nightingale often told the nurses under her charge, "so it is for us to care for their feet as well as for their wounds."

She made note of the dead soldier's name and the time of his dying. Later, she would update the records she so meticulously kept on her patients, and would send the dead man's scant possessions home to his family, along with a personal note reassuring his parents that he had died peacefully. She covered his face with the blanket, knowing that before morning call it would be covering another miserable wretch perhaps also doomed to die in Turkey. It was long past midnight by the time Nightingale finished making her nightly circuit through the 4-mile maze of the Scutari Barrack Hospital. She could not, of course, personally tend to each of the thousands of patients whose miserable fate it was to be lying in those stinking corridors, but it was later said that as the Lady with the Lamp passed by, soldiers lying in those corridors would kiss her shadow.

"We must do better than this," Nightingale wrote in her personal journal before crawling onto the soldier's cot that was her bed. And do better she did. By the time the Crimean War had ended, Florence Nightingale established the first hospital pharmacy, using her own funds to purchase needed medications. She recruited a French chef to start the first hospital nutrition service, and instructed her nurses to begin boiling sheets, cloths and rags, simultaneously creating the first hospital laundry and infection control process. To give her patients something to do other than spend their army pay on drink, she established the first patient library, and she personally took responsibility for assuring that the money they saved was sent home to their families. Her meticulous recordkeeping was the forerunner to the medical records and epidemiology functions of the modern hospital. At the Scutari Barrack Hospital, Florence Nightingale drew up what was effectively a blueprint for the hospital as we know it today. As Mark Bostridge wrote in his recent biography *Florence Nightingale: The Making of an Icon*: "By the end of the war, the Scutari hospitals had been transformed into efficiently-organized, smooth-running operations."

Nightingale largely disappeared from public view upon her return to England, but her work did not end there. She personally helped each of the nurses who had gone with her to Turkey find employment upon their return home. She was the guiding light for the world's first school of professional nursing, which to this day bears her name, and her book *Notes on Nursing* informed and inspired future generations of nurses. She designed the first hospital building that was constructed specifically for that purpose. The pioneering epidemiological methods she developed were the basis for revolutionary improvements in the British military health service, and she was a leading proponent for public health improvements in what was then the British colony of India. She was a dedicated advocate for preventative health, and for the healthcare rights of soldiers and veterans.

More than sixty years after the Crimean War, the children of an old soldier who was a veteran of that war were making final arrangements for his funeral. Among his possessions they found a shriveled old orange, no bigger than a walnut. With the orange was a note scribbled on a scrap of paper that read: "Given to me by Miss Florence Nightingale." When Nightingale herself was buried, her coffin was attended by octogenarian veterans of the Crimean War, one of those countless conflicts that have blighted the history of human progress, and which would have been forgotten by history but for the work of the Lady with the Lamp, Florence Nightingale.

We must do better than this. *One day early in the twenty-first century, Florence Nightingale decided to come back and see how we were doing.*

CHAPTER ONE

"Mommy! Mommmmmmy!!" It was three o'clock in the morning and 10-year-old Timmy Mallory was dying. They had not told him he was dying. Not really. Not yet. But he'd known for about a week. He could tell by the way everyone was acting, by the way they all treated him. The chemotherapy was not working and the doctors were not going to save him. He was going to die. The nightmares had become more terrible and more frightening every night. "Mommmmmmy!!"

"Shh," whispered a soft voice. Timmy felt hands gently rubbing his temples. They were a woman's hands, he could tell, and though they were rough and calloused, the touch was tender and reassuring. "Shh, my brave little soldier." Timmy wanted her to tell him that everything would be alright, the way his mother always did, but he knew it wouldn't be true. She kissed him on the forehead and continued softly rubbing his temples. "Sleep now, my brave little soldier."

Timmy smiled as he drifted back into sleep. In his dreams, he rode a magnificent white charger off to do battle with the fire-breathing dragons that were trying to kill him. He was a brave soldier, and he would not surrender lightly. Florence Nightingale kissed her brave sleeping soldier on the top of his bald head, then picked up her lantern and continued making her rounds through the corridors of Memorial Medical Center. How very different this place was from the Scutari Barrack Hospital. And how very much the same.

Carol Jean Hawtrey sipped her vanilla latte, nibbled her cinnamon bagel and smiled to think that hospital food had come an awfully long way since her days as a young nurse. She was reading a front-page newspaper article about the healthcare crisis. "Let's see now," she asked herself, "just when did the healthcare crisis become a crisis? Was it with the latest capital crunch and reimbursement cutbacks? Or was it the evolution of managed care and corporate medicine? Does the crisis go back to the establishment of Medicare, which was still revolutionary when I was in nursing school? Or all the way back to the Hill-Burton Act after the Second World War? Actually, those were each a response to the healthcare crisis of their own era." She closed up the newspaper with a smile. Having written a book about it, she knew that between 1854 and 1856, Florence Nightingale and her small team of nurses had transformed the Scutari Barrack Hospital into the forerunner of the modern medical center. That, too, was a response to the healthcare crisis of Nightingale's day. And the healthcare crisis would, in one form or another, still be with us far into the future.

After having spent more than twenty years as an ICU nurse and another dozen on the nursing school faculty, having sent two kids off to college and careers of their own, having gotten divorced and learned how to live on her own again, Carol Jean had been looking forward to retirement. Then she'd decided to write a book. *Leadership Lessons from Florence Nightingale* had improbably led her into a third career as a healthcare consultant. And that work had led her to be here, in the Memorial Medical Center cafeteria, on the first day of her latest client engagement.

Sipping her latte, Carol Jean tuned in to the conversation at the next table. Five employees in hospital scrubs had been gossiping and complaining for the past quarter-hour – now they were talking about the new fountain the hospital had recently installed in the healing garden courtyard, visible through the cafeteria windows. "They should have put the money in our paychecks instead of squandering it on a CEO ego trip," one of the nurses said as the others nodded in agreement.

"Mind if I join you?" Carol Jean didn't wait for permission to pull her chair over. *Proceed until apprehended* was a philosophy she'd picked up from her study of Nightingale's way of getting things done. "I heard you talking about the fountain – it's beautiful, isn't it?"

"A beautiful waste of money that has nothing to do with patient care," one of the nurses replied.

"Oh, I don't know," Carol Jean said, "when I came in this morning there were several patients sitting by the fountain who seemed to be enjoying it very much."

"Not as much as I'd enjoy a pay raise," another of the nurses said, and they all laughed, Carol Jean included.

"I've yet to meet anyone who wouldn't be happy with a pay raise," Carol Jean said, "and no doubt thinks they deserve it. Probably does deserve it for that matter, but financial reality always has a way of rearing its ugly head."

"Yeah, well financial reality certainly hasn't kept the suits from giving themselves big pay raises." Despite her brightly-flowered scrubs, the nurse who said this had immediately struck Carol Jean as being one of the surliest people she'd seen in quite a while. Carol Jean tried to read the name on the nurse's badge, but the lanyard upon which it hung was twisted so the badge was backwards. Carol Jean made out the letters I-CARE, which she knew were printed on the back of every nametag. "I-CARE," she said, "isn't that an acronym for Memorial Medical Center's values?"

The nurse looked down at her badge without bothering to turn it around. "Actually, it's 'why care?' We're doing more with less, you know, so who's got time to care?"

This one's going to be a challenge, Carol Jean thought to herself as the nurse in the floral scrub shirt glared at her, arms crossed, from the other end of the table. "By 'the suits' I assume you mean the executive staff," Carol Jean asked. The nurse sipped her coffee and nodded slightly. *She has the bearing of a natural leader – for better or worse*, Carol Jean thought. "And you think they're overpaid?" The surly nurse just laughed, and the others joined in. "I take that as a yes," Carol Jean said with a smile.

Carol Jean leaned forward and placed her forearms on the table, fingers interlaced in front of her. "Did you read the article in the newspaper this morning about the healthcare crisis? About how brutal the competition is between hospitals, about how many of them are having to make painful cutbacks, and some have even been forced to shut their doors?"

The nurse with the backward nametag replied, "Yeah, we saw it. So if times are so tough, how can they find the money to build a glitzy new fountain?"

Carol Jean returned the nurse's stare. "Let me ask you a question. You've seen the billboards and heard the radio ads from the hospital across town – your competitor – right?" No one needed to respond – St. John's Hospital had placed a billboard right across the street from the MMC patient parking ramp. "And you know the surgeons are planning to build their own ambulatory surgery center out in the suburbs, right?" Several of the nurses nodded – everyone had heard that particular bit of scuttlebutt. "And you've heard that hospitals might not be paid at all for taking care of patients if something goes wrong?" They'd certainly heard that one; so-called "never events" had been the subject of mandatory in-services over the past several months. "And that's just the tip of the iceberg, isn't it? We could add the nursing shortage, regulatory compliance issues, turmoil in the capital markets and a whole lot more, couldn't we?"

"Are you going to get around to that question you wanted to ask us?" The nurse in the floral scrubs, whom Carol Jean was increasingly certain that by virtue of a dominant personality rather than official title held great sway among her coworkers, leaned back in her chair, arms still tightly folded across her chest, frown firmly fixed on her face.

"Yes I am, and here it is. In the environment I've just described, where the very survival of Memorial Medical Center – oh, and by the way, all of your jobs – is at stake, do you really want the hospital board to hire the cheapest CEO they can find from the bargain basement of some outplacement firm? Is that who you want leading your hospital into the future? A cut-rate CEO?"

"That's not what we're saying." It was the nurse to Carol Jean's left. Her name badge was correctly positioned – Francine from the Emergency Department.

"Well," Carol Jean replied, "I apologize, but it sounded an awful lot to me like you were saying that the suits, as you called them, are overpaid." As one, the nurses crossed their arms and leaned back in their chairs with cynical frowns fixed on their faces, subconsciously mimicking the body language of the surly nurse in the floral scrubs. "Listen," Carol Jean said, "I sympathize with you, I really do. I spent many years – more years than I can count – as a floor nurse. And all the things you're complaining about, I used to bitch about those same things."

"So tell us why you're here." The nurse in the white scrub shirt, who had not yet said a word, eyed Carol Jean suspiciously.

"I'm here because your CEO invited me. I'm a healthcare consultant." Carol Jean thought back to the call she'd received several months earlier from John Myerson, MMC's chief executive officer. He was concerned that the medical center's staff and patient satisfaction scores were stuck in the bottom quartile of their comparison groups, and that so far nothing they'd done had seemed to have much of an impact. His chief nursing executive, who'd read *Leadership Lessons from Florence Nightingale*, had suggested that he call Carol Jean. But Carol Jean didn't mention any of that, saying only, "I work with hospitals on a program called *The Florence Prescription*. Though it's really more a way of life than it is a program or a prescription. It's my answer to the question 'what would Florence Nightingale do?' if she were to come back as a consultant to the modern hospital."

"You're the one who wrote the book?" The nurse with the floral scrubs and the reversed nametag leaned forward and rested her chin on a closed fist.

Carol Jean was quite proud of her book, and not a little surprised at how well it had done, but still was a bit embarrassed when the book put a spotlight on its author. "Yep, that's me."

The frown softened slightly and the nurse, now looking more skeptical than angry, leaned forward. "So, what are you going to tell the suits Florence would do for us?"

Carol Jean shrugged, "Nothing at first. Right now, I really don't know enough to tell them anything they don't already know. My first job is to ask good questions, then to listen and think."

"Well, I hope they let you out of the executive suite so you can get around and talk to some of us peons up on the floors."

Carol Jean nodded. "You can bank on it – it's in my contract."

Francine from the Emergency Department looked over at the surly nurse and pointed to the watch on her wrist. "Well, ladies," the nurse in the floral scrubs said, confirming Carol Jean's impression that she was the group's informal leader, "time's up. Back to the salt mines." The nurses all started to push away from the table.

"Before you go," Carol Jean said, "do you all meet here every day at this time?"

"Only on Mondays."

"Well, can I join you next Monday? I think by then I'll have some more questions for you." The nurses looked back with expressions ranging from skeptical to defiant. "You told me I should get out and talk to people," Carol Jean said as she stood up. "So I'd like to talk with you. I'll even buy the coffee."

> You can't be cynical and negative sitting in the cafeteria or break room and then somehow flip an inner switch and become genuinely caring and compassionate when you walk into a patient's room. And patients see right through the fraud.

"That won't be necessary," said the nurse with the backwards name badge.

"Okay, so I'll see you next Monday," Carol Jean replied, ignoring the snub. "What's your name?"

"Ask me next week," the nurse replied, looking back over her shoulder as she started toward the cafeteria doors.

Carol Jean pushed her chair back over to her original table and sat down. "Well, Miss Nightingale, it looks like we really have our work cut out for us, doesn't it?"

"Her name is Sarah Rutledge," said Florence Nightingale as she sipped her tea and watched the group disappear through the cafeteria door. The chair in which she was seated had been vacant the second before. Other than Carol Jean, nobody in the cafeteria seemed to notice her presence.

Carol Jean looked from Nightingale to the closed cafeteria door and back again. "If this group is representative, I can see why MMC is struggling with patient satisfaction scores. You can't be cynical and negative sitting here in the cafeteria and then somehow flip an inner switch and become genuinely caring and compassionate when you walk into a patient's room. And patients will see right through the fraud."

"She is one of the best nurses in this hospital, that one with the flowered blouse is. I've watched her care for my brave little soldier upstairs. You need to win her over, Carol Jean. You need her to fight *with* you, not against you. Win her over and the others will follow."

"I think that's going to be a real challenge," Carol Jean replied, shaking her head.

"No bigger challenge than convincing a British doctor at Scutari to wash his hands before sawing off the leg of some poor wretch whose misfortune it was to have taken a bullet for the Queen," Nightingale said with an impish smile. "And there's a brave little soldier upstairs whom we can enlist in the campaign."

CHAPTER TWO

"You must be Carol Jean. We've been looking forward to your visit." The young woman stood up, came around from behind her desk, and extended her right hand. "I'm Connie O'Dell, John's executive assistant. I'll let him know you're here." John Myerson had been CEO a bit less than three years, and during that time had brought a new sense of urgency to Memorial Medical Center, whose very survival had been in question in an increasingly competitive urban marketplace.

"So you're the power behind the throne," Carol Jean said as they shook hands. "We all know how helpless CEOs would be without their executive assistants."

"Yes, but I still let him think that he's running the show," Connie said in a conspiratorial whisper.

Connie was young, not much past college graduation, Carol Jean guessed. She had the winning combination of a cheerleader's smile and the professionalism expected of an executive assistant in a major medical center. "I'm a bit early. Do you mind if I ask you a few questions before we tell John I'm here?"

"Certainly. What would you like to know?"

"In my role as a consultant, how do you think I can be most helpful to John and the leadership team? In other words, what problem keeps them awake at night that I might be able to help solve?

Connie laughed. "You say that as if there's just one thing keeping them awake at night! The bond issue for the new building, challenges from the medical staff, trying to get enough nurses to staff the floors, uncompensated care, a fractious governing board, take your pick. If that's not enough, I can give you the next five things on the list." Connie crossed her arms and leaned back against the desk. *I hope Myerson takes good care of her*, Carol Jean thought, knowing that some of her other CEO clients would hire a person like Connie in a heartbeat if they met her.

"What would be at the top of *your* list, Connie?"

Connie pinched her chin between her thumb and forefinger of the right hand, and rested her right elbow in the palm of her left hand. "Good question. Right now, I'd have to say employee morale. We're doing a lot of exciting things, but I think people are really feeling the stress, and frankly some of their bad attitudes just make it worse."

Carol Jean was about to ask another question when Myerson emerged from his office. Carol Jean had spoken with him on the phone, and of course done all the research consultants usually do on new clients, but she was still surprised by how young he looked. He was, she guessed, not quite six feet tall, with the sparse frame of a distance runner. Brown hair with a tinge of grey at the temples was capped by what appeared to be an untamable cowlick at the crown. He had the winning smile of a TV game show host, but looking closer the wrinkles around his eyes betrayed too much worry and too little sleep. He had a fat file folder in his hand, and was obviously not prepared to see Carol Jean standing there. Connie took the folder and said, "John, this is Carol Jean Hawtrey here for her ten o'clock appointment."

"Oh, yeah, that's right," he said, looking at the clock on the wall. "Great to meet you, Carol Jean. I'll be just a minute if that's okay. Would you like a cup of coffee?" he asked as they shook hands.

"I'm all set," Carol Jean replied. "Connie is taking good care of me." Carol Jean examined the framed motivational posters hanging on the reception area walls while Myerson spoke with Connie. When they'd finished, she followed him into his office. Every square inch of wall space was covered with renderings and blueprints of the new building. "Construction begins next spring," Myerson said, obviously excited about it. "People are really looking forward to having more space."

"We've come a long way from Scutari, haven't we?" Carol Jean asked the question as she studied the artist's rendering of the medical center's new entrance.

"Excuse me?"

"Oh, sorry. Scutari was the place in Turkey where Florence Nightingale established the first hospital – at least as we'd recognize the term today."

"Oh, yeah, I remember reading that in your book, which I really enjoyed by the way. Grab a chair, and let's try to clear a little working space." Myerson's round table was also strewn with blueprints and spreadsheets, which he stacked into a reasonably neat pile. After they'd made the usual small talk Carol Jean said, "So tell me, what would you say's your biggest challenge today? What challenges keep you awake at night?"

"That's easy," Myerson replied. "Getting this new building paid for." He looked into his coffee mug as though there might be a pile of money down there, then took a sip.

"I see. What about people issues? Do they interfere with your sleep?"

"Of course they do. That's why you're here."

"I'm happy to be here, and looking forward to working with you." Carol Jean took a long look over at the door. It was closed. "Oh, by the way, I don't know if I mentioned this, but I'll have a partner working with me. She's going to add an awful lot, but she's a very private person. We'll to have to keep her involvement strictly a secret between the two of us."

Myerson nodded and took another sip of coffee. "That's fine with me. I'm open to all the help we can get. I'll look forward to meeting her."

"Well, she's right here. John Myerson, meet Florence Nightingale."

Nightingale had just appeared in the third chair. She was wearing a plain black dress with a white lacy collar, hair pulled back under a simple bonnet. Myerson nearly fell over backward in his chair, and spilled coffee all over the table. "Oh dear," Nightingale exclaimed as she pulled a cloth from one of the deep pockets in her dress and began mopping the spilled coffee, "this just won't do." Looking over at Carol Jean she laughed and said, "I do seem to have this effect on people." Myerson rubbed his eyes long and hard with the heels of his palms, and when he opened them again he clearly expected to see that Miss Nightingale would be gone. "Still here," she said with a sprightly giggle.

Myerson got up from his chair and walked quickly over to the window. Arms crossed, he stared out at the parking lot. Several times he looked back over his shoulder and each time Nightingale was there, smiling back at him. After the third time he stalked across the floor toward his desk, muttering as though he'd seen a vandal's handiwork scrawled across one of his new buildings. He reached for the phone. "There's no need to call Security, John," Carol Jean said. "Come back over and join us. I can explain." Myerson leaned on his desk with both arms extended and a suspicious look on his face. "Come on, John, just flow with this. You'll be glad you did. Really."

After glaring long and hard at Carol Jean and Florence Nightingale sitting there at his table Myerson finally, and with obvious reluctance, came back around and took his seat. "So tell me, what is this all about?" He looked even more pointedly at Nightingale. "And who are you?"

Nightingale didn't respond, but instead looked to Carol Jean. "She is who I said she is, John. Though the historical Florence Nightingale died a hundred years ago, her spirit has remained as a living presence in healthcare ever since. And now, in ways that I cannot understand myself, much less explain, she's come back in a more real way to help us work on reanimating that spirit – which I'm afraid is at risk of being lost. She won't be with us for long, so we should make the most of the time while she is."

Before Myerson had a chance to reply, Nightingale looked over at the renderings that were taped up on the wall. "I was a bit of an architect myself, you know, Mr. Myerson. Tell me about your new hospital." For the next 15 minutes Myerson, still in a state of shock, walked his two guests through the schematic drawings on the walls. Nightingale stopped him frequently with questions. "If the nurses cannot see all the patients from their station, how do they know if someone needs help? With all these walls, you can't possibly have cross-ventilation, so how do patients get fresh air? Where is the dormitory for your nurses?" She listened carefully as Myerson explained the technological infrastructure of the modern medical center.

When they'd finished their virtual tour of the unbuilt hospital, they returned to the round table. "This will be a beautiful hospital," Nightingale said as she took her seat. "You must have wonderful architects."

Myerson nodded. "Yes we do. I've worked with them before and they really understand how to create a patient-centered environment."

"Of course, whether or not a hospital is – what did you call it? – patient-centered? – really has very little to do with the design of the buildings and everything to do with the invisible architecture of what's inside. Wouldn't you agree?" She looked at Carol Jean with pursed lips and said, "Patient-centered care? Is there any other kind?" Then she looked back at Myerson. "What are you doing to design the invisible architecture that will be inside the physical structure of your new hospital?"

> Invisible architecture is to the soul of your organization what physical architecture is to its body. Invisible architecture, not the buildings, determines whether you are a good hospital, a great hospital, or just another hospital.

It took Myerson a moment to realize the question had been directed at him. Finally he said, "Until about ten minutes ago, I would have considered that to be a silly question. But tell me what you mean by invisible architecture." Then he looked over at Carol Jean. "Didn't I read something about that in what you sent to me?"

Carol Jean nodded. "Yes. Miss Nightingale and I have been working on this notion for quite some time now." Myerson looked back over at Nightingale and then, almost as if afraid to look for too long, quickly turned his gaze back to Carol Jean. "You see," Carol Jean continued, "the first impression patients, visitors, and prospective new employees have of Memorial Medical Center will be created by your physical facilities: the landscaping in the parking lot, the glass and red brick fronting the building, the new fountain in the courtyard. But that won't be even the slightest consideration when patients are asked whether they were happy with their care, or if one of your valued employees is considering a job offer from somewhere else. Will it?"

Myerson took a quick look back at Nightingale, who nodded her encouragement, then replied, "Probably not."

"Invisible architecture is to the soul of your organization what physical architecture is to its body," Carol Jean said. "And it's the invisible architecture, not the buildings, that determines whether you are a good hospital, a great hospital, or just another hospital."

"When I arrived at Scutari," Nightingale added, "our tasks were obvious and immediate. Basic sanitation, nutrition for the soldiers, getting the orderlies to do their jobs rather than tipping their mugs and chasing after my nurses. It was hard work, but at least we could see and measure our progress. And the real measure of that progress was that fewer soldiers died. The harder task was getting everyone to work together like the horses in a team rather than wild beasts each running with their own wills. Getting them to think of their patients' needs before tending to their own comforts. In that, I'm afraid I was not very successful at Scutari."

"Miss Nightingale is much too hard on herself," Carol Jean interjected. "But the thing she's talking about – building a cohesive team that puts patients first – is more a function of invisible architecture than it is of buildings, policies and procedures, and all that other left brain stuff. Not just at Scutari, but in her subsequent work with reforming the British military health service, establishing nursing as a profession, and so much else, she was largely successful because she convinced others to take ownership for the goals she established."

"Carol Jean makes it sound as if I did it all myself," Nightingale said with a dismissive nod, "but in truth many hands contributed to the work at Scutari. Without my dear friend Mother Mary Clare Moore and the sisters of Bermondsey Convent, all would have been for naught. But for the politics of religion and the vagaries of history, it would have been her statue and not mine in Waterloo Place. I learned from her that leaders must often follow those whom one is supposed to be leading. Indeed, when there is a culture of ownership, leaders are often followers and followers are often leaders."

Carol Jean nodded her assent. "And that, I believe, is the most important challenge facing hospitals today. You foster a more committed and engaged workforce when people have a sense of ownership for the organization. And whether or not people are committed and engaged will profoundly affect productivity, customer service, and employee morale. At our leadership retreat on Friday, we'll go through eight characteristics that are essential for fostering a culture of ownership."

"Okay," Myerson said as he leaned forward and looked from Carol Jean to Nightingale and back again, "but I'm a bottom line sort of guy. I don't want to wait until Friday – give me the executive summary."

"Alright," Carol Jean replied, "let's begin with the ultimate goal we discussed on the phone. You want a more positive and productive organization with a more engaged and committed workforce where patients really are at the center of the care matrix. Accountability alone won't get you there. You can hold people accountable for showing up on time and for fulfilling the terms of their job descriptions, like parents checking a report card, but you cannot hold them accountable for being

> You can hold people accountable for showing up on time and for fulfilling the terms of their job descriptions, but you cannot hold them accountable for being committed and engaged. You cannot hold people accountable for caring. It takes a spirit of ownership for those things to happen.

committed and engaged. You cannot hold people accountable for caring. It takes a spirit of ownership for those things to happen. So let's go over the eight essential characteristics required to foster a culture of ownership. These characteristics are mutually reinforcing – they build upon one another – and to one degree or another, you've got to have all eight if you're really going to an organization where people hold themselves accountable because they've internalized that spirit of ownership."

Myerson leaned back in his chair and picked up a yellow pad and a pen from his desk, then returned to the round table. Carol Jean waited for him to finish scribbling a few notes at the top, then continued. "The first characteristic common to organizations with a culture of ownership is commitment – people buying-in to the hospital's values, vision and goals. And that commitment is reflected in the second characteristic, which is engagement. People who are thinking like owners aren't mentally somewhere else as they go through their day's work, they're present head and heart, not just hands. And owners are passionate about what they do – passion is the third characteristic. When there's a culture of ownership, you can feel the enthusiasm almost from the time you walk in the front door. Ralph Waldo Emerson said that nothing great was ever accomplished without enthusiasm, and he was right. Our patients deserve to have us bring our best game to work every day."

Carol Jean steepled her fingers and closed her eyes for a moment. The reason she'd begun to study the life and work of Florence Nightingale in the first place was a nagging sense that these first three characteristics – commitment, engagement and passion – had been swallowed up by the healthcare crisis. She felt it herself, every day she went to work, the sense that the spirit of purpose and mission that had once galvanized Nightingale to make such a total commitment to her patients was missing. Her research had taken her to London to visit the Florence Nightingale Museum. She was standing at the foot of Nightingale's statue in Waterloo Place when she heard a soft voice say, "You're going to need some help, dear." That was the beginning of her extraordinary relationship with Florence Nightingale.

Carol Jean opened her eyes again and saw Myerson looking at her expectantly. "People who are committed, engaged and passionate take initiative, which is the fourth characteristic. If they see a problem, they either fix it or refer it to someone who can fix it; they never say 'not my job.' But more than that, owners are always thinking of ways to make things better, not just fix problems. Someone with the owner attitude will stay at a hotel and see the staff there do something they like, then come back and say 'that was really cool – let's do it here at Memorial Medical Center.' They are the spark plugs who power your organization into the future." Carol Jean paused for a moment as Myerson finished making a note. "In a similar manner, people tend to be better stewards of things they own than they are of things they rent, and stewardship is the fifth essential characteristic. So promoting a spirit of ownership is also an investment in productivity and cost-effectiveness."

Commitment — to values, vision and mission

Engagement — being fully present, physically and emotionally

Passion — loving your work and letting it show

Initiative — seeing what needs to be done and taking action to get it done

Stewardship — effectively shepherding limited resources

Belonging — being included, feeling included, and including others

Fellowship — being a friend and having friends at work

Pride — in your profession, your hospital, your work, and yourself

"The next one is, I think, a bit more challenging. Florence and I really struggled over whether to call it inclusion or belonging, and settled on the latter because owners don't just feel included, they feel like they belong – belonging is the sixth characteristic. But to create that sense of belonging, leaders must begin by doing more to make people feel included. The benefit of doing that is you'll also promote a greater spirit of fellowship, which is the seventh characteristic. I'm sure you're familiar with the Gallup data which shows that a key determinant of employee engagement is whether they have friends on the job."

Myerson finished writing then looked up from his notes. "You know, I'm very proud of the people at MMC, but looking at these characteristics I also see that we have a lot of work to do. And that we have a pretty incredible opportunity. You said there are eight characteristics. So far, I only have seven."

"Well," Carol Jean replied, "you just mentioned the eighth. It's pride. Owners take pride in their work, in their professions, in their organizations and in themselves. Pride is the natural outcome of successfully cultivating the first seven characteristics."

Myerson turned a page in his yellow pad and printed the eight characteristics then scribbled a few words behind each one. Then he turned the pad around so it was oriented toward Carol Jean. "Like this?"

Carol Jean read the notes and nodded. "You got it, John. But as I've said, culture rests on a foundation of core values. I'll tell you what, why don't we take a walk and talk a bit more about values."

"Okay, but what are people going to say when they see…" Myerson looked over to the chair where Nightingale had been sitting, but there was no one there. "Where did she go!"

"Don't worry, John," Carol Jean said as she stood up. "She went upstairs to prepare her brave little soldier for our visit."

"What brave little soldier? What visit?"

"Let's go for a walk. There's someone I'd like you to meet."

CHAPTER THREE

"I promise I'll get you back in time for your next meeting," Carol Jean said as she started for the door. Myerson looked wistfully at the pile of blueprints and spreadsheets as he reached for his nametag. "Why don't you leave that here, John."

"But it's policy. Everyone has to wear one, even..."

"Not today," Carol Jean interrupted, shaking her head. "Just humor me on this for now, okay? But we'd better get moving if we're going to get you back in time for your project steering committee. Connie said it's at eleven, right?"

Myerson nodded, looked around his office once more, as if to make sure none of Nightingale's friends had popped in unannounced, then followed Carol Jean out into the reception area. She stopped at Connie's desk and picked out four red M&M's from the candy dish. "Project steering at eleven," she heard Connie remind Myerson as he followed her toward the main first floor corridor. They walked down the main hallway past the gift shop, the outpatient pharmacy, and the cafeteria. Just beyond the main corridor intersection, Carol Jean stopped at the elevator and pushed the "up" button. After they'd waited thirty seconds or so, Myerson cleared his throat. "One more reason we need that new building – efficiently get people where they need to go."

On the elevator, Carol Jean hit the button for the eighth floor. "Twenty-seven to two," she said.

"Twenty-seven to two what? Do you bet on horse races?"

"Not as such," Carol Jean said with a smile. "Out of the twenty-nine employees we passed on our way to the elevator, only two even acknowledged us. Don't you have a rule of some sort that people are supposed to smile and say hi? Especially to visitors? Or, one would think, to the CEO?"

"Yeah, well, you know how it is when people get busy. I'll have the training department schedule another in-service on our see-smile-greet-help rule."

"See-smile-greet-help rule?"

Myerson looked slightly peeved as he explained. "When passing someone in the hallway, the rule is that you're supposed to see and acknowledge them with eye contact, then smile and say hello, and if they look like they're lost or need help, stop and offer your assistance. That's the rule anyway."

"That's the problem with rules," Carol Jean said as they exited on the eighth floor. "They only work on the left side of the brain." She glanced at the directional signs for Pediatric Oncology, then paused to look out the plate glass window at the courtyard below. "That is a lovely fountain. It really adds something special to your healing garden, don't you think?"

Myerson joined her at the window. "Absolutely. What do you mean, rules only work on the left side of the brain?"

"You know the distinction, don't you, between the left brain and the right brain?"

"Refresh my memory."

"Left brain is linear and analytical. Right brain is nonlinear and relational. Left brain is the bean-counter. Right brain is the poet. The left brain counts and the right brain matters. That's one of the central themes we'll be covering as we work together. An organization that's all left brain is boring; an organization that's all right brain is chaos. Part of the art of

> The left brain counts and the right brain matters. Part of the art of leadership is knowing how to balance, and how to integrate, left brain discipline and right brain creativity.

leadership is knowing how to balance, and how to integrate, left brain discipline and right brain creativity. Most hospitals today are way over-developed on the left side of the brain. Too many rules."

Myerson crossed his arms and frowned, keeping his eyes on the courtyard eight floors below. "You've got to have rules. Otherwise, like you just said, you'd have chaos."

Carol Jean leaned against the handrail, her weight resting on both arms, and smiled at the sight of a mother chasing her toddler around the fountain. "Rules are of the left brain, values are of the right brain. When people don't share a common set of values, you need to have lots of rules." She looked at Myerson and smiled. "The IRS comes to mind." Looking back down at the healing garden, she continued. "If people don't value being friendly, you have to give them rules telling them to smile, and a script that tells them what to say. As if people can't come up with 'have a nice day' on their own."

Myerson glared down at the fountain. "Yeah, well, you can't teach people values. If they didn't pick them up at home, they're not going to pick them up here."

Carol Jean looked at Myerson, her eyes popped open and her jaw dropped in mock surprise. "Really now? Is that true, that you can't teach people values? Why, I just saw you doing it."

"What do you mean, you saw me doing it?"

"Twenty-nine to zero."

"What?"

"We passed by twenty-nine people in the first floor corridor and you didn't see-smile-greet or help a single one of them."

"I was talking to you."

"Oh, is that in the rule? You're excused if you're talking to someone else?"

Myerson turned toward Carol Jean, arms even more tightly crossed, and for a second she wasn't sure if he was going to say "You're right" or "You're fired." They stood there like that, the CEO and the consultant, in a staring contest. Finally, Myerson smiled and stuck his hands in his pockets. "I guess what you're saying is that I wasn't doing a very good job of teaching our values as you and I were walking down the hall."

Carol Jean laughed. "John, people can choose whether or not to follow rules, but their values will always shine through in how they treat others. I probably should have told you this before. I make my living as a consultant, but I earn my keep as an insultant, telling clients things they need to know but don't want to hear. Don't take it personally."

Myerson pursed his lips and shook his head. "No, Carol Jean, I am going to take it personally. On the way back to the office, my see-smile-greet-help ratio will be twenty-nine yes and zero no, and if it's not, I want to hear from you."

"That's something you can take to the bank, John. It's not in my nature to keep my mouth shut. But please don't miss my key point. The values that you deem to be core – whether they spell out I-CARE or something else – must be more than words on a plaque stuck up on the wall. If you and your people do not know and live those values, then they're just good intentions, nothing more. Values are the foundation of your invisible architecture. They, more than anything else, define who you are. Your core values – and I emphasize that these are the values that you *decide* are core – define what you stand for. And what you won't stand for." She turned her back to the window and gave Myerson a nudge on the shoulder. "Come on, let's go meet our brave little soldier."

The nurse's station for Pediatric Oncology was a beehive of activity. The unit clerk was typing at her computer, phone receiver pressed between her shoulder and her ear. "One minute," she mouthed as she continued tapping the keys. After hanging up, she looked at Carol Jean, then John. "Can I help you?"

"Yes," Carol Jean replied, "we're here to see Timmy Mallory."

"Are you family?" She looked at Myerson in the manner of someone trying to place a vaguely familiar face.

"No, we're friends." Carol Jean looked over at the CEO and arched her eyebrows, then looked back at the unit clerk. "Timmy should be expecting us."

"One minute." The unit clerk got up and walked over to a nurse standing at the back counter reading a chart. It was the nurse in the flowery scrubs from the cafeteria – the one Nightingale had said was named Sarah Rutledge, who was one of the best nurses in the hospital. She took a quick look at the two visitors, gave a curt nod, then turned her attention back to the chart. The unit clerk returned and said, "Timmy's in Room 819, but he's on restricted visitation. We're trying to make sure he gets his rest, so you can only stay for a few minutes." She pointed down the hallway to the left of the nurse's station. "Sixth door on the left."

As they walked down the corridor, Carol Jean tugged on Myerson's suit coat sleeve. "It's been a while since you've been up here, hasn't it? I guess managing by walking around is a rule and not a value, huh?"

Myerson stared straight ahead. "Point made," he said as they stopped at the door for Room 819. Inside the room, Timmy Mallory was bouncing up and down on the bed, wielding a yardstick like a broadsword, engaged in what appeared to be a fight to the death with his IV pole. A vicious slash to the throat sent the IV pole crashing to the floor, taking Timmy's IV line with it. The catheter ripped away from his arm, and blood spurted all over the bed. "Victory!" Timmy shouted as he swung the yardstick over his head, blood droplets creating a ring of concentric circles around him on the bed. Pumping his left fist in the air and pointing the yardstick at the fallen IV pole with the other he shouted, "The white knight prevails, evil dragon, wounded but victorious!"

Sarah Rutledge came rushing into the room, pushing her way past Myerson and Carol Jean. "Timmy, what on earth are you doing?" She glared at the two adults as if they had instigated the whole riot. Turning back to Timmy she said, "Give me that stick, young man, and lie back down in that bed." She turned off the stopcock and angrily ripped the catheter from the end of the tube. "You two are going to have to wait," she said as she marched over to the supply cabinet and drew a new catheter from one of the drawers. Timmy looked over at the two visitors, shrugged, and smiled a twelve-dollar smile.

After restarting Timmy's IV, Sarah steamed past Carol Jean and Myerson. "Please try not to get him all riled up again." Carol Jean was surprised that, even as angry as she was, she gently pushed the door shut behind her. And Myerson was stunned to see Florence Nightingale suddenly standing on the far side of Timmy's bed.

"Did you see the way my brave little soldier dispatched that hideous dragon to an early and well-deserved grave," Nightingale said with obvious pride. Timmy beamed triumphantly.

"Timmy," Nightingale said, leaning down toward him, "this is Mr. Myerson and Miss Hawtrey. They came up to say hello."

Timmy looked at Carol Jean, smiled and said hi. Then he fired a stare at Myerson. "Is this the guy you were telling me about?" Nightingale nodded her assent. Timmy never took his eyes off Myerson. "So are you, like, the boss of all the nurses?"

Myerson stuffed his hands deeper into his pockets and shrugged. "I guess you might say that, Timmy. Are they taking good care of you?"

"Oh, yeah, they're all really good. Except, you know, when I make too much noise killing dragons and stuff."

Myerson laughed. "Well, we certainly can't have dragons in the hospital, Timmy, so you keep on killing them."

"I will," Timmy replied solemnly. "But there's an awful lot of them."

"And a good thing that my brave little soldier is here to vanquish them all," Nightingale added.

Timmy looked back at Myerson. "You're the boss of all the nurses?" Myerson again shrugged and nodded. "Then you need to give them a pay raise," Timmy said with a surprising air of authority.

Myerson arched his eyebrows, gave Nightingale a suspicious glance, then looked back at Timmy. "Why do you say that, Timmy?"

"Sometimes I hear them outside my room. They say 'I don't get paid enough for this,' and stuff like that. So you should give them a pay raise." Nightingale laughed, pointed to her chest and shook her head to say that she had no part in Timmy's campaign to get the nurses a pay raise.

"Well, Timmy," Myerson said, "we try very hard to make sure everyone who works here gets paid fairly. But I'll tell you what. When I get back down to my office, I'll ask someone to check and make sure we're where we need to be. Okay?"

Timmy nodded. "Okay."

Myerson looked toward the foot of the bed, but Nightingale was not there. He rubbed his eyes, shook his head and looked again, but she was still gone.

"She went down to the chapel," Timmy said nonchalantly. "That's where she goes to think."

CHAPTER FOUR

"After leaving Timmy's room, Carol Jean and Myerson walked past the nurse's station, now vacant except for the unit clerk talking on the phone. "The chapel's on the second floor, right?" Carol Jean asked. Myerson nodded. "While you go to your project steering committee meeting, I think I'll go have a chat with Florence."

"Do you really think she'll be in the chapel?"

"If she's anywhere in the hospital, that's where she's most likely to be."

"Think she'd mind if I join you?"

"What about your project steering committee?"

"Judy can handle it. She's our Chief Operating Officer."

"Actually, I think Florence would be disappointed if I showed up without you."

Myerson pulled the cell phone from his pocket and called Connie to let her know the change of plans. He didn't tell her they'd be in the chapel, only that he did not want to be interrupted unless it was urgent. "Let's go," he said.

The chapel was a cozy little room tucked away behind the physical therapy department on the east wing. "Cozy" was Myerson's expression for anything he thought was too small and needed to be replaced by the new building project. The cozy ICU, the cozy cafeteria, the cozy parking ramp – all slated for replacement. "So," Carol Jean asked as they rounded the last corner, "is the cozy little chapel getting a home in the new building?"

"Not in the current plan," he said, "but I think that might change before the end of the day." Myerson held the door for Carol Jean and they entered the chapel. It was indeed cozy, with three small rows of pews and a handful of chairs in the back. Nightingale was sitting in one of the chairs, eyes closed and hands folded in her lap. Sensing their presence, she opened her eyes and motioned for them to join her.

"When I was young," she said, "I always believed that for one to just sit idly, to just sit thinking and dreaming, was such a ghastly waste of time. But now, I quite enjoy it. Tell me, has my brave little soldier gone back to battling dragons?"

"I think they were trying to make him take a nap," Carol Jean answered.

"Hmm. I see." Turning to Myerson she asked, "Is there a hospital rule that children should not slay dragons in their rooms?"

"Not as such," he replied, "but I think I'm seeing some opportunities for our pediatric areas. The next project after the new wing goes up is a dedicated children's hospital. Maybe we need to include a special dragon-slaying arena on every unit."

"That would make Timmy happy," said Nightingale.

"If he's still here," Carol Jean said. "Didn't you tell me that the doctors had given up hope?" Even as she heard the words coming out of her mouth, she regretted saying them.

"Just because the doctors have given up hope doesn't mean there's no longer hope. An American contemporary of mine – Emily Dickenson, a poet – have you heard of her?" They both nodded and Myerson muttered "of course." Nightingale continued. "She wrote a poem in which hope is a bird perched in your soul singing a song that needs no words. Timmy is listening to that little bird. Whether he will be here for your new children's hospital, only God knows, but hope never dies."

They sat quietly for a few minutes and even Myerson, who rarely sat still long enough to warm a chair, seemed comfortable with the silence. At last Nightingale asked, "Did you two speak further about the invisible architecture of the hospital?"

Myerson nodded. "Briefly. We talked a bit about core values, and how that is the foundation of the invisible architecture."

"Yes," said Nightingale, "and the extent to which people live those values will determine whether you are building on a foundation of rock or on a foundation of sand. What did you notice about the nurse who came running into Timmy's room?"

Myerson shrugged. "She was in a hurry?"

"That she was. The instant she heard the commotion, she dropped whatever she was doing and came running. But why was she running like that? Because she loves Timmy, my brave little soldier. You can see it in the gentle way she puts the catheter in his arm, the way she always rubs his head before she leaves the room. That is compassion, which I believe is the "C" in your I-CARE values." Myerson nodded. "What else did you notice during our short time with Timmy?"

"Well," Myerson laughed, "he certainly is an exuberant kid."

"That he is," replied Nightingale. "And observant as well. *You should give your nurses a pay raise,*" she said, perfectly mimicking Timmy's voice. "Where do you suppose he got that idea – which he most certainly did not get from me."

"I imagine he overheard some of the nurses complaining in the corridor."

"Yes, and that's not all he's heard" Nightingale said. "Two of the letters in your I-CARE formulation stand for Integrity and Respect. When patients overhear caregivers complaining and gossiping, it violates the integrity of the caregiver and shows a lack of respect for the patient, not to mention the person who's being complained or gossiped about. The message the patient receives is that you're not really serious about the values in I-CARE. If people don't live them, all the time, they are just good intentions, little more than suggestions."

Carol Jean turned her chair to more directly face Myerson. "The reason I say that values are the foundation upon which you build the culture of your organization is because the values your people live – which may or may not be the ones plastered on the backs of their nametags – profoundly influence your organizational culture. Every organization has a culture – it is to the hospital what personality and character are to the individual. Your culture will be defined by what you expect and by what you tolerate. And over time, what you tolerate will dominate what you say you expect. To permit is to promote. If you *permit* people to deviate from integrity, compassion and respect – for example, by passing gossip in the hallways and break rooms, whether or not there happens to be a patient within earshot – you will inevitably *promote* a culture where those values are just good intentions. With I-CARE you tell people that you *expect* them to act with integrity and to treat people with compassion and respect, but if you *tolerate* gossip and rumor-mongering you insidiously undermine those values."

> Culture is to the hospital what personality and character are to the individual. Your culture will be defined by what you expect and by what you tolerate. Over time, what you tolerate will dominate what you say you expect.

"Well," Myerson said, "every hospital runs on the rumor mill. And I'm not really sure that there's much we can do about changing culture. That's sort of a given, at least in the short run."

"When we spoke on the phone," Carol Jean replied, "you told me that you don't want Memorial Medical Center to be like every other hospital. You want it to be the best; you want it to go from good to great. But if your culture is not consistent with your core values, you might possibly be good, but you will never be great. And so not only can you influence the culture, you *must* if you are to achieve that goal of being the best."

Nightingale had been staring at the stained glass artwork through which no light passed because it was suspended on a brick wall. With a long blink, she ended her reverie and rejoined the conversation. "At Scutari, most of the orderlies were lazy ne'er do-wells. They wouldn't go near the sickest patients, they wouldn't help change dressings on the most hideous wounds, they wouldn't stoop to empty the chamber pots." She looked to Carol Jean then back to Myerson. "You have no idea the smell of a hospital where the chamber pots are not frequently tended. That was the culture of Scutari, and it was the culture of the

British military healthcare system. It was a culture that was deplorable and intolerable."

"So what did you do?" Myerson asked.

"Exactly what Carol Jean is saying that you need to do. We raised our expectations of those men – and the orderlies *were* all men, I might add – and then we became less tolerant of their failures to meet those expectations."

"Yes," Myerson pressed, "but *how*? How did you get them to change their behavior? What did you do that made things different?"

"A good question," Nightingale replied. "The first thing we did was to make clear our expectations. Until then, if orderlies did a proper job of taking care of the officers, they were free to lie about, to drink, and to chase after my nurses. We had to make clear to them that we now expected them to help in the care of every soldier, not just the officers, and that they were to busy themselves with helping on the wards, including emptying the chamber-pots, rather than flirting with the nurses."

Nightingale shuddered as if wracked by some ancient and painful memory. "At first, they just laughed at me. So it was not enough for me to lay out those expectations once. I had to do it every day, both in words and in action. Tell me, Mr. Myerson, have you ever told the people of this hospital that you *expect* them to stop complaining about problems and work on fixing those problems? Have you ever told the people of this hospital that you will *not tolerate* them spreading rumors or talking about other people behind their backs?"

"Uhm, well, not in so many words."

"If you haven't told them in so many words, then you haven't told them at all."

Myerson looked over at Carol Jean. "Is this what you meant by being an insultant?"

"Being a what?" Nightingale asked, somewhat indignantly.

"I'll explain it later," Carol Jean said with a wave of her hand. Turning to Myerson she said, "Another of the values in I-CARE is accountability. Part of what Florence is saying is that it's not enough to just hold people accountable for what's in their job description. You also have to hold them accountable for the attitudes they bring to work with them, and for the way they treat each other. If you don't do that, then you're not holding yourselves accountable as a management team. That's just one of the ways that the *structure* of culture builds upon the *foundation* of core values in your invisible architecture."

Myerson crossed his arms defiantly, a posture that was belied by an engaging smile. "Now you've both become insultants. You're ganging up on me!"

The ladies both laughed and Carol Jean said, "No we're not, John, we're teaming up *with* you. For us to do our part on that team, we have to be honest with you. Let's go back to culture for a minute. What was your first reaction when we walked into Timmy's room and you saw him engaged in fierce combat with his IV pole?"

"Honestly, I was horrified," Myerson replied, "and I immediately had a picture of Gloria Hoffmann pop into my head. She's the attorney who would defend us in a negligence suit if he'd fallen off the bed and hurt himself."

"And how did his nurse respond to Timmy's rambustiousness?" asked Nightingale.

"Oh, I think she was just as horrified as I was, though probably for different reasons. One of which, admittedly, might have been that the hospital's CEO was in the room."

"Did it ever occur to you," Nightingale said, "that vanquishing that IV pole was every bit as important to little Timmy's fight against cancer as all of the sophisticated medical treatments he's enduring?"

Myerson thought for a few seconds then slowly shook his head. "No, I really hadn't thought of it that way."

"Nor had his nurse, evidently," Nightingale said.

"When we spoke on the phone," Carol Jean said, "and I asked you about the type of culture you wanted here at MMC, the first words out of your mouth were 'patient-centered.' I've seen those same two words in all of your promotional materials."

"And you will continue to. That is our top priority."

"If you were *really* patient-centered," Carol Jean said, "what would you have done, what would Timmy's nurse have done, upon coming into that room and seeing him jumping on the bed having a make-believe sword fight with a make-believe dragon?"

"I suppose we would have found a safe place for him to play," Myerson replied. "And given him more IV poles," he added with a chuckle.

"Do you know what your nurses need even more than a pay raise, Mr. Myerson?" Nightingale leaned forward, resting her forearms on her thighs and looking as if she were about to finally disclose the secret meaning of life. Myerson scratched the side of his nose and looked expectantly, but didn't answer. "They need for you to give them permission to care."

Myerson narrowed his eyes and pursed his lips. "I'm not sure I'm with you on that. Can you say more?"

"I think what Florence is saying," Carol Jean interjected, "is that you owe it to your people to define cultural expectations that are consistent with your core values. Compassion is one of your core values. Productivity is *not* one of your core values. But – don't deny it, John, because you know it's true – your nurses are getting a very clear message that they will be held accountable for productivity first and for compassion second. If you are truly serious about compassion as a core value, if you really mean it when you use the words 'patient-centered' in your promotional materials, then you must give your nurses permission to express real compassion. Permission to take time out to play with a sick child, or to read a story to an elderly patient, even if it means they fall short of their productivity targets for that day. Permission to let a little boy take his dragon fights out into the hall where he won't hurt himself, even if visitors, or the occasional hospital administrator who happens to be passing through, look askance at it. Even if it gives your hospital lawyer a panic attack."

"You see, Mr. Myerson," Nightingale added, "creating the right culture is nothing more and nothing less than knowing who you are, knowing who you want to be, and then doing the things you must do in order to become that which you want to be. People would have a lot more time and energy for compassion if they spent less time and energy complaining and gossiping."

"That's the challenge." Carol Jean sighed and looked over at the stained glass hanging on the wall, then back at Myerson. "Building culture requires simultaneously placing restrictions on behaviors that detract from the ideal, and encouraging behaviors which reinforce that ideal. Even if those behaviors – like letting your patients go out into the hallway to slay their dragons – are quite different than what you would expect at an ordinary hospital. In fact, the more unique you are, the better. That's why hospital culture is your only sustainable source of competitive advantage. No competitor can copy your culture the way they can copy your business practices, and no competitor can steal your culture the way they can steal away your doctors and nurses."

Myerson's cell phone rang before he could say anything. "Myerson," he snapped as he flipped it open. He turned to apologize to Nightingale for the interruption, but she was no longer in the chapel with them. He barely managed to not drop the phone onto the floor.

"John, sorry to bother you, but Dr. Warren is here and says he needs to speak with you right away." Carol Jean could hear that it was Connie on the other end of the line. Miles Warren was a general surgeon and, as far as Myerson was concerned, a general pain in the neck. A crisis like being unable to find an open space in the doctors' parking lot would have him in Myerson's office threatening to move his entire practice across town – a threat Myerson had nearly taken him up on more than once.

"I'll be down in a minute. Feed him some of your M&Ms and ask him about his new Jaguar so he'll be in a better mood by the time I get there, would you?" Myerson snapped the cell phone shut and stuck it back into his pocket. "Duty calls," he said, "but before I go down to face the wrath of Dr. Dracula, I'll walk you over to Ginny Latroia's office. Ginny is the head of our volunteer services program. She's going to give you the nickel tour this afternoon." He looked down at Carol Jean's feet, then back at her face. "I hope you brought a pair of running shoes."

Carol Jean laughed. "I'm afraid high-heeled sneakers aren't an approved element of the consultant's wardrobe. But I'll try to keep up with her anyway."

CHAPTER FIVE

"Will Florence be joining us?" Myerson felt vaguely ridiculous asking if one of the patron saints of healthcare, a woman who had been dead for a century, would be joining him and his recently-retained consultant for the meeting they'd scheduled in his office as a wrap-up on her first day at Memorial Medical Center.

"Probably not, though you can never be sure when she'll decide to pop in. She told me she planned on spending some time alone in the chapel and then, after things had quieted down on the floors, visiting her brave little soldier in Pediatric Oncology." Carol Jean picked out one of the four blue M&M's she'd taken from Connie's candy dish on the way in and popped it in her mouth. It was 6:30 in the evening and they were the only two left in the executive suite.

"Well, it's been quite a day," Myerson said after heaving a big sigh. "Nothing at all like what I expected it would be! What are your impressions so far?"

"It's really too early for me to venture any impressions, John. Give me until the end of the week. Something Florence keeps telling me – you can never listen too much and you can rarely talk too little." She looked at the typed page that spelled out her itinerary for the following day. "It looks like I'll have plenty of opportunities for listening tomorrow."

Myerson laughed. "As soon as people heard that a famous author was coming to work with us, they all wanted to be on your schedule. If it gets to be too overwhelming, just let Connie know and she'll scale it back for you."

"It won't be a problem, John. I believe in immersion consulting. But let's talk a bit more about values and culture before we call it a day. Okay?"

Myerson extracted an empty yellow pad that was buried amidst the pile of blueprints, pulled a pen from his shirt pocket, and scribbled a few tight circles in the upper left-hand corner of the page. Carol Jean watched as he wrote her name, the date, and the words "Initial Recap Meeting" at the top of the page. When she'd started her practice five years earlier, a friend had told her that a good consultant, like a good salesperson, needs the ability to read upside down. "Tell me more about the invisible architecture," Myerson said. "Should we be thinking about it for the management retreat on Friday?"

Carol Jean finished her last blue M&M and organized her thoughts. "Yes, and probably with most of the focus on culture. But right now, let's go back to your core values. As I said this morning, core values are the essential foundation for your hospital's invisible architecture. If you were to make a list of all the possible words and combinations of words that might be included in a hospital's statement of values, which I have done, there are more than 500 different possibilities. So the first question is why did you choose the values that are in *your* statement of values? Was it because they spell out a cute acronym like I-CARE – or was there a deeper reason for the choices you made?" Carol Jean noticed Myerson writing down MMC's core values – Integrity, Compassion, Accountability, Respect and Excellence – and wondered how many MMC employees actually knew them by heart.

"Why did you choose accountability? Why not responsibility? Why respect rather than dignity? Why didn't you include anything related to stewardship of resources or effective financial management, when rising healthcare costs are widely perceived to be a problem of near-crisis proportions? And why, given that recruiting and retaining good staff will be your biggest challenge in the years to come, is there no reference to loyalty in your statement of values. Isn't that something you should value today, especially with the huge amounts of money you're spending for traveling nurses?" She paused for a minute to let Myerson catch up with his note-taking. "What process did you go through to assure that the five values designated for MMC are aligned with the personal values of your employees, so they feel a sense of ownership for those values and not like they're just words on the back of a name badge? Failing that sense of ownership, they're more likely to say 'why care?' than 'I-CARE,' and in fact some of them already do."

"Whoa, slow down there," Myerson pleaded as he struggled to keep his pen moving as fast as Carol Jean was talking. "I can't answer most of those questions for the simple reason that I inherited these values. The plaque was there on the wall of the lobby the day I walked in for my first interview."

Carol Jean nodded thoughtfully. "So the question is whether the MMC values statement is like the Ten Commandments, immutable for all time, or more like the U.S. Constitution, amenable to amendment as warranted by circumstances. What do you think?"

Myerson doodled on his yellow pad. "I'm not really sure. I-CARE has been around for a long time, and a lot of people have bought into it. Or at least gotten used to it. As my consultant, what do you think?"

Carol Jean smiled at the way Myerson had pulled one of the oldest consultant tricks in the book – answer a question with that question. She replied with the second-oldest trick in the book – respond to a question with an analysis instead of an answer. "First off, let's look more deeply at your current statement of values, only one of which is really a value."

Myerson arched his eyebrows and tapped his pen on the table. "What do you mean, only one of our values is really a value?"

"At a personal level, a core value is a deeply-held philosophical commitment to a pattern of attitudes and behaviors that determines how you think, how you set goals and make decisions, how you develop relationships, and how you deal with conflict. Integrity – the 'I' in

> At the personal level, a core value is a deeply-held philosophical commitment to a pattern of attitudes and behaviors that define and shape how you think, how you set goals and make decisions, how you develop relationships, and how you deal with conflict.

I-CARE – is a core value because it implies an unshakeable commitment to honesty and reliability, and to honoring the dignity of every individual. The root of the word integrity is integer, meaning an undivided whole, or as Florence would say, we are all children of the same God. And it means being effective stewards of our resources, because whatever we waste is not available to our neighbors or our children. So you see how all-encompassing a core value is. The cornerstones of Integrity are honesty, reliability, humility and stewardship. If people are not committed to those behaviors, then integrity is just a word on the back of a name badge, not a core value."

Myerson unconsciously turned over his name badge and read the MMC values. Carol Jean continued. "At the organizational level, a core value should define your non-negotiable expectations regarding how your people behave, the goals toward which you direct your collective efforts, and how you work together within the organization. So for the organization to select 'integrity' as a core value implies that you will expect your people to act with integrity – as defined by the four cornerstones I just mentioned. It also means that as an organization you will establish practices that systematically institutionalize integrity. That means everything – from how you bill Medicare to the way you treat patients in the emergency department on a busy Saturday night – must pass your organization's integrity test. Otherwise it's just a word. Enron had the word integrity in its statement of values, but that's all it was. Just a word."

> At the organizational level, a core value should define your non-negotiable expectations regarding how your people behave, the goals toward which you direct your collective efforts, and how you work together.

Myerson wrote the word INTEGRITY in all caps, and underneath wrote the four cornerstones in another bulleted list. Next, about halfway down the page he wrote "Personal Integrity" on the left side and "Organizational Integrity" on the right side. Then he drew a bidirectional arrow between the two:

Personal Integrity ⟷ Organizational Integrity

"I never really thought about the fact that integrity needs to be defined in two different ways," Myerson said, "one for the individual and one for the organization, but it makes a lot of sense. I also see how the two interact with each other. If you have an organization like Enron that fosters a culture of greed and dishonesty, even good people can be influenced to act in ways that lack integrity. And unless you vigilantly guard against it, the failure of a small number of individuals to act with integrity can cause the entire organization to descend to the lowest common denominator – an Enron sort of climate where integrity is defined merely as not getting caught rather than not doing wrong in the first place."

Now Carol Jean was making notes. "That's a profound insight, John. I really hadn't thought of it that way either. But you're right – there *is* an ongoing interaction between personal and organizational values. Let's explore that as we go along."

Myerson nodded as he scribbled "MMC ≠ Enron" on his yellow pad. Then he said, "What about the other four? You said they aren't really values. Can you explain what you mean by that?"

"I will. But first, another important distinction – between values and things you value. I value having a clean car and money in the bank, but those are not values, they are outcomes. They are determined by my behaviors. If I go to the car wash and am disciplined about my spending, I will achieve those outcomes. In the same way Excellence – the 'E' in I-CARE – is not a value, it's an outcome. It depends upon a certain set of behaviors, which will be specific to every outcome for which you desire excellence. The behaviors required to achieve the outcome of excellent chicken soup in the hospital cafeteria will be different from the behaviors required to achieve the outcome of excellent results in cardiac surgery."

"That makes sense," Myerson said as he made a few more notes on his pad. "So what about the other three – Compassion, Accountability and Respect?"

"What do you think? Let's take respect. Is that a value?"

"Well, it is certainly something we value. To use your earlier terminology, we should expect people to treat each other with respect, and we should not tolerate people treating others with disrespect."

"So does that make it a value? Or is it a behavior? Or an outcome?"

Myerson closed his eyes and leaned his chin on his two closed fists. "Hmm. It's really both a behavior and an outcome, isn't it? To treat someone with respect is a pattern of behavior, but to earn their respect is an outcome."

"Bravo, Professor," Carol Jean exclaimed. "And more than anything, you earn the respect of others by living your values – values like integrity. How about compassion? Value, behavior or outcome?"

Myerson scratched his cheek and tapped his pen. "Well, it's really sort of a feeling. You know, feeling empathy for someone."

"Like the feeling you get walking by a homeless person on the street?"

"Yeah, like that," Myerson said with a nod.

"Even if you don't do anything about it? Even if after your brief compassion attack you keep on walking without dropping any coins in the cup. Is that really compassion? Or more specifically, would that pass the I-CARE test for compassion – say, in the E.D. on a busy Saturday night? Just feeling sorry for someone without doing anything about it?"

"No," Myerson said with an emphatic shake of the head. "Clearly not."

"So when you get right down to it, compassion is a behavior."

"Yes, when you get right down to it," Myerson repeated, "compassion is a behavior."

"So where does that leave us with Accountability? Value, behavior or outcome?"

"Hmm. That's a tough one. It could be a behavior or an out-come."

"But not necessarily a value?"

Myerson frowned and doodled some more, then shook his head no. "Well, Carol Jean, you've done a pretty good job of whittling down our statement of values, haven't you. Let's see, we're down to – hmm, just one. Integrity."

Carol Jean laughed. "Let me clarify. A statement of values can very appropriately contain behaviors and outcomes that you value. But it's important that you see where they fall on the Values – Behaviors – Outcomes continuum."

Myerson scratched it out on his pad, then asked, "Like this?"

Values → Behaviors → Outcomes

"Exactly. Let's look at a specific example. Last year your overall turnover rate was more than twenty percent, and several of your med-surg units are now operating with almost as many temps as regular nursing staff. So reducing turnover would be a valued outcome, wouldn't it?"

"I'll say!"

"But we're really not talking about turnover per se, are we? That's just a symptom of a deeper problem. The desired outcome is not reducing turnover, it's increasing loyalty. You want to earn people's loyalty, not just lock the door so they can't leave. So once you've defined that desired outcome, what behavior changes are required to achieve it?"

Myerson leaned back in his chair and looked at the ceiling. "Man, where do we even start?"

"That's right!" Carol Jean exclaimed. "Where do we start? How about this: start by asking why people leave. Regardless of what they might tell you, people usually don't leave for more money; often it's simply because they don't get along with their direct supervisor. If that's the case, what behavioral changes would it suggest you work to bring about?"

"The first thing that comes to mind is doing a better job on performance appraisals. Too many of our managers don't take the process seriously. Most people want to know how they're doing. They'd rather have honest feedback that's critical than hear nothing at all, or to be given a superficial pat on the back."

"So what's that tell you?"

"That we haven't been clear about our expectations. We haven't educated managers how to meet those expectations, enabled them with the tools they need to do the job, energized them to continuously

The 6-Es of Employee Engagement

1. Expect   4. Energize

2. Educate   5. Evaluate

3. Enable   6. Elevate

monitor their subordinate's progress toward achieving agreed upon goals, and then evaluated how they're doing."

"Very good," Carol Jean said with a knowing smile. "Expect, Educate, Enable, Energize and Evaluate."

"I read your book," Myerson replied.

"Then you remember the sixth, and most often overlooked, 'E' in *The 6-E's of Employee Engagement.*"

Myerson furrowed his brow and touched both temples with his forefingers in mock concentration. "Wait, don't tell me, it will come to me."

"Instead of taking the stairs…"

"Elevate! Celebrate to Elevate. That's the sixth E. You elevate people by using the performance appraisal process to celebrate their growth and successes, and also their good faith failures, and not just as a way to dole out pay raises."

Carol Jean nodded, obviously pleased that Myerson had read her book carefully enough to recall her formula for employee engagement. "And what *organizational* core values would encourage your managers and supervisors to practice the 6-E's?"

"In our formulation, the most important one would be Accountability – managers holding themselves and their people accountable for high expectations. But the process would need to be carried out with compassion and respect, with a mutually-committed goal of achieving excellence."

"And that's a great example of how values interact with one another. Accountability without respect creates parent-child relationships; a culture of ownership demands adult-to-adult relationships. Tomorrow, let's talk more about culture, and how it's built on the foundation of values. I'll also want to discuss some ideas about moving from a culture of accountability toward a culture of ownership. And we'll get into cultural blueprinting, which is the next step in crystallizing your invisible architecture."

"Well, dear, the secret of accountability is actually quite simple. You never give an excuse and you never take an excuse." Neither Carol Jean nor Myerson had seen the door open because it hadn't, but Florence Nightingale was now standing beside them at the table. "I attribute any success I might have achieved during my lifetime to that one principle. Now, if you two are finished with your business here, I would like to show you something."

Carol Jean looked at Myerson. "I think we've done enough for today. Should we still plan on getting together first thing in the morning?"

"Let's make it eight-thirty," Myerson replied. "I meet with the surgical staff at seven." Myerson stood up and bowed slightly as if being introduced to royalty. "Good evening, Miss Nightingale, it's a pleasure to see you again."

"Trust me, Mr. Myerson, mine is the greater pleasure in being seen. But if you would come with me, there is something else I would like you to see." Myerson reached for the suit coat jacket that was draped across the back of his chair. "You won't need that, Mr. Myerson," Nightingale said. "No one will see us tonight."

Myerson shook his head in disbelief, but before he could say anything he found himself standing at the entrance to Pediatric Oncology, flanked by Carol Jean Hawtrey and Florence Nightingale. "Come with me," Nightingale said and started down the hallway. Neither the unit clerk nor the doctor who was in the nurse's station working on a chart took note of their passing. She led them to Room 819, the room that for too much of his young life little Timmy Mallory had called home.

Timmy was fast asleep. There was a woman sitting on the edge of his bed, singing softly. Though she was now in street clothes, Carol Jean recognized her. It was the nurse in the floral scrubs. The surly nurse she had met in the cafeteria. Thirty minutes beyond the end of her shift, Sarah Rutledge was perched on Timmy's bed singing him a lullaby.

And she was crying.

CHAPTER SIX

Since her meeting with Myerson was not until 8:30, Carol Jean decided to go to the hospital cafeteria for an early breakfast and catch up on her reading. It was 6:30, and the place was nearly deserted. Carol Jean stocked her tray with coffee, a bagel and a banana, paid the cashier, and scanned the dining area. At a table in the far corner, sitting all alone looking out the window and nursing a cup of coffee, was the nurse in floral scrubs, the surly nurse, the nurse that Nightingale had told her was named Sarah Rutledge and was an excellent nurse. The nurse who, on her own time, the evening before had sung Timmy to sleep with lullabies while she sat on the edge of the bed and cried. "After half a night's sleep she's back for another shift," Carol Jean said to herself. "I'd be grouchy too."

"Mind if I join you?" Carol Jean laid her tray on the table but did not sit down.

Sarah stared at her for several seconds, then looked back out the window. "It's a free country. Sit anywhere you want."

Carol Jean hesitated for a moment, then pulled up a chair and sat down. She sipped her coffee in silence as she too looked out the window at the healing garden. And the brand new fountain.

"You're still pretty upset about that fountain, aren't you?" Sarah didn't answer, just crossed her arms tight against her chest and scowled. "I saw you up on your unit yesterday," Carol Jean said, taking a new tack. "Mr. Myerson and I came up to visit one of your patients. Timmy Mallory. What a nice young man."

Sarah kept her arms crossed and her eyes fixed on the fountain as she replied. "Yeah, I saw the two of you up there. It's a good thing Myerson had you with him. Otherwise he'd have gotten lost."

"I take it you don't see him on your unit very often."

Without moving her chair, Sarah twisted her torso to face Carol Jean. "In the past three years, I've seen Santa Claus on our unit three times. Yesterday was the first time I ever saw Myerson up there. So on Pediatric Oncology, Santa Claus is more real than our CEO."

"So do you think one of my consulting recommendations ought to be that administrators should spend more time making rounds up on the units?"

"What would Florence do? Isn't that the question you kept asking in your book? I think that, instead of squirreling herself away in a cushy conference room talking about more ways to squeeze more money out of nursing, Florence would be up on the floors asking how she could help. Don't you? Not just once every year or so, like when the Joint Commission or some out-of-town consultant happens to show up. Every day. Maybe if they did that, the suits would realize we need new IV poles and wheelchairs more than we need that fountain out there."

Carol Jean resisted the temptation to defend Myerson and his team. "Is that what you would tell Mr. Myerson if he walked up to the unit and asked you what you need? That you need basic stuff like wheelchairs and IV poles?"

Sarah yanked her chair around to face Carol Jean. From the look on her face, Carol Jean wasn't sure if she was going to scream or cry. "I'll tell you what I'd tell him," Sarah replied with scarcely controlled anger. "I'd tell him that I have two kids in college, that my husband has been out of work for the past four months and is losing hope that he'll ever find anything, and that every credit card I have is at the limit. I'd tell him that every time I hear one of the suits chanting that BS 'do more with less' mantra, I want to shove the words right back down his throat because you know what? I don't have any more in me to do more with less." Sarah leaned forward with her hands on her knees and her eyes bored into Carol Jean. "I'd tell them to stop feeding us that I-CARE slogan, because that's all it is. A slogan. The day a suit walks up to the unit and asks me what he can do to help my husband find a job, or helps me get the credit card goons off my back, *if* that day ever comes – and trust me, it won't – on that day I'll start believing they care. But until they show me they care, tell me, why should I go out of my way to make them think I care about their silly slogan?"

Sarah took a deep breath, leaned back in her chair, stretched her legs out in front of her, and shoved her hands into the pockets of her scrub pants as she stared defiantly at Carol Jean. After a very long and very uncomfortable silence Carol Jean softly asked, "What would they have to do to show you they really do care?"

"The suits?" Sarah snorted contemptuously. "They could help me with my kids' college tuition. Put that in your report. Don't you think Florence would have done something like that? Before we built that fancy fountain out in the courtyard?" Sarah looked over at the clock on the wall – quarter to seven. Carol Jean knew she didn't have much time to end the conversation on a positive note. She sipped her coffee and looked out the window at the fountain, then back at Sarah.

"If Florence Nightingale was sitting here right now," Carol Jean said, nodding toward the empty chair on the other side of the table from Sarah, "what would you say to her?"

"Florence… Nightingale… is… dead," Sarah replied, truculently emphasizing each word.

"I know that," Carol Jean said with a smile. "I wrote a book about her, remember? But humor me. If you had a chance to speak with her, just one chance, what would you talk about?"

Sarah rolled her eyes. "Is this what the hospital pays you consultants to do? Ask people ridiculous questions?"

"Humor me. What would you say to her?" Sarah shook her head with evident disgust, then looked back at the clock. "I gotta go to work." She started to push herself away from the table while picking up her paper coffee cup.

"I think I know what she would say." Florence Nightingale was suddenly sitting in the chair next to Sarah. She had a grey shawl draped over her shoulders but otherwise was in the same simple black dress and white bonnet from yesterday. Sarah fell back in her chair and dropped a half-full coffee cup, which bounced off her foot before puddling on the floor. Nightingale looked down at the spilled coffee and gave Carol Jean a sly wink then said, "I think Sarah would say that taking care of the sick should be a mission, not just a business, and that being a nurse or any other health professional should be a calling, and not just a job. I think she would say that amidst the fancy buildings and the endless paperwork and the doctors' parking lot filled with expensive cars and all of the – what do you call them, Sarah? – the 'suits' being so busy designing the visible architecture for their next building that they can't see that the invisible architecture is in serious need of repair, I think she'd say with all of that, our hospitals are at risk of losing their souls. That's what I think she would say. Am I correct, Sarah?"

> Taking care of the sick should be a mission, not just a business. Being a healthcare professional should be a calling, not just a job. Our hospitals are at risk of losing their souls.

Sarah stared at Nightingale, her mouth slightly open and completely oblivious to the hot coffee that was working its way through her shoes and into her nylons. "Is this some sort of joke," she said at last, in a half-whisper.

"No, Sarah, it's not a joke," Carol Jean replied. "You are now an official co-conspirator in our effort to re-spark the soul of healthcare in this country, beginning right here at Memorial Medical Center. Welcome aboard."

"I don't... want to be a... co-conspirator in anything," Sarah mumbled, shaking her head and still unable to take her eyes off Nightingale.

Nightingale nodded sympathetically. "In 1854, it would have been so much easier for me to remain at home in the quiet comfort of Lea Hurst. I could have lived out the life of a pampered spinster, whiling away the hours with my beloved books and long walks in the English countryside. It was a much harder road, the one I took to Scutari. I had to forget the desires of Florence Nightingale and remember the needs of the soldiers I was called to serve. That, dear Sarah, is the path of the nurse."

Sarah blinked hard, looked from Nightingale to Carol Jean, then shook her head and blinked again. She looked around the cafeteria, but nobody else seemed to sense anything out of the ordinary. "This can't be real."

"You will come to appreciate that reality is a reasonably malleable notion," Nightingale said. "And compared to my Doctor Menzies," she said, turning to Carol Jean, " you Mister Myerson is a saint."

"What we are working toward, Sarah," said Carol Jean, "is nothing less than a revolutionary transformation in the culture of this hospital. But I can't do it for you, not even John Myerson can do it without the help of people who are committed to positive change. Despite what you've been trying to tell me, you do care, don't you? In fact, Sarah, you care so much it hurts. That's why you're hiding behind this mask, pretending to be so negative, so cynical. Because it hurts too much to care, it hurts too much to hope. I'm right, aren't I?"

Sarah's lip trembled and she fought back tears. Now it was just the two of them, Sarah and Carol Jean, sitting at the table. The clock still read 6:45. "That wasn't real. That didn't really just happen."

Carol Jean shrugged. "What does your heart tell you? Do you want for it to be real?"

Sarah looked down at the spilled coffee on the floor, and wiggled her foot. "Oh sh…" The expletive trailed off into the air.

"Listen, Sarah, last night Florence and I watched you singing for Timmy Mallory."

Sarah's eyes narrowed and she glared suspiciously. "You what?"

"It's true. You couldn't see us, but we watched you. If you don't believe me, I can tell you the name of the lullaby you were singing, the color of the sweater you were wearing. It was yellow. This *is* real, Sarah. The opportunity to be part of a change like this is so rare. We need you, Sarah. We need your help to make this happen."

Sarah looked at the clock and pushed back her chair. "It will never happen. You know why? Because the suits won't let it happen. They have the power and they have the money and they just don't care."

Carol Jean leaned forward and touched Sarah's knee with her fingertips. "It wasn't just Florence and me watching you singing to Timmy." Sarah's suspicious glare became more intense. "John Myerson was there, too."

Sarah scowled. "You had better tell me that's not true, Ms. Big Shot Consultant. You had better say that you didn't bring the CEO up to spy on me."

"No, we didn't bring the CEO up to spy on you, Sarah. He needed to see you and Timmy – Florence calls Timmy her brave little soldier. He needed to see the two of you there to open his heart to the difficult things we're going to be telling him he has to do."

"I don't believe you," Sarah said, barely constraining the fury in her voice.

"It's true, Sarah. And one more thing you should know. It wasn't just you crying in that room last night. John Myerson was crying, too."

CHAPTER SEVEN

Sarah stared at the chair where Nightingale had been sitting, obviously trying to convince herself that it had been vacant all along. Then she looked back down at her coffee-soaked shoe and shook her head. "I gotta go to work... but now I have to go change my shoes first." She looked back at the empty chair and shook her head. Then she walked away without looking back. Carol Jean sipped her coffee as Sarah disappeared through the double doors of the cafeteria.

"Well, Ms. Hawtrey," Carol Jean said to herself, "that was either a perfect ten or a belly-flop. And you probably won't know for a while." She couldn't decide whether to study her notes or walk around the hospital and explore, and instead ended up just having two more cups of coffee as she gazed at the fountain and allowed her thoughts to roam. At 8:15, she returned her tray and walked down the hall to the administrative offices.

"Morning, Connie. Beautiful day, isn't it?"

"I'll say! I actually thought about playing hooky – calling in sick and going for a bike ride instead of coming to work." Carol Jean feigned shock and Connie hurriedly added, "But I obviously resisted the temptation. John was expecting you, but Dr. Warren barged in unannounced about ten minutes ago. Would you like some coffee while you wait?"

"No thanks, Connie. Any more coffee and I'll float away. But I will take a few of these." Carol Jean picked out four yellow M&Ms from Connie's candy tray. "My favorite color," she said somewhat sheepishly as she put the first one in her mouth. At that moment, Myerson's door swung open and out marched Dr. Warren, looking like he'd been sucking on a dill pickle. He steamed by without acknowledging either Connie or Carol Jean.

Myerson emerged several seconds later and leaned against the door frame. "Two men are arguing about who is privileged to sit in the doctor's lounge," he said with a wry smile. "One is speaking Swahili and the other is speaking Mongolian, so neither has a clue what the other is talking about. So they compensate by talking louder. Who wins the argument?" Connie and Carol Jean looked at each other and shrugged. Myerson looked from one to the other then said, "The one who laughs first." When neither woman seemed to get it he added, "Because he's the one who appreciates how absurd the entire argument is, and absurdity is the lowest form of comedy." Myerson extended his right hand to Carol Jean. "Sorry to keep you waiting. Come on in."

"So, how was your morning?" Myerson asked as they sat at his round table. Carol Jean replied that she'd enjoyed several varieties of coffee down in the cafeteria, but did not mention the conversation with Sarah, or the fact that one more person at MMC had now experienced the presence of Florence Nightingale.

"Getting back to the invisible architecture of your organization," Carol Jean said, "yesterday we covered core values. This morning, let's explore how corporate culture is built upon that foundation of core values." Myerson nodded his agreement, and turned the yellow pad to a new page. "Every organization has a culture," Carol Jean continued, "though in many cases that culture has evolved haphazardly rather than by conscious design."

"When I was in graduate school," Myerson said, "one of the professors was adamant in insisting that leaders can no more change the culture of an organization than they can change the weather. But yesterday you said that should be my top priority. So how does a poor CEO figure out who's right?"

Carol Jean pursed her lips and nodded. "Good question, but your professor was wrong. You *can* blueprint corporate culture. In fact, it's a paramount leadership responsibility for several reasons. First, your culture says a lot about who you are as an organization. As I said earlier, culture is to the organization what character and personality are to the individual. To say that it can't be influenced is every bit as nonsensical, and ultimately self-sabotaging, as for the individual to say that self-improvement efforts are a waste of time, and that personality and character are immutably fixed."

Myerson made a note on the yellow pad. "I guess you could say the same thing about a family, couldn't you? Parents are responsible for helping to mold the personality and character of each individual child, but also for creating a positive and nurturing 'culture' within the family."

"Good point, and I'm going to steal it. T.S. Eliot said good poets borrow but great poets steal; I do both! I hadn't thought about the parallel between an organization and a family, but you'll see it in my next book – of course, crediting you in the acknowledgments." Myerson shrugged as if to say that wouldn't be necessary. "The other reason it's essential for leaders to manage culture is that over time, it's your only sustainable source of competitive advantage. Everything else can either be copied, the way your cross-town rival recently copied your women's health initiative, or stolen, the way an out-of-state hospital stole away your director of radiology last month. Because it must be authentic and deeply internalized, a great culture can neither be copied nor stolen."

> Every organization has a culture, though in many cases that culture has evolved haphazardly rather than by conscious design. Culture is the only sustainable source of competitive advantage, and cultural blueprinting is more important than designing buildings.

"Okay," Myerson replied, "I can't disagree with anything you've said. So how do we go about crafting the culture we want?"

"Well, as I said yesterday, you start by making sure your cultural blueprint is laid on the solid foundation of core values. So let's take a look at several specifics. The 'A' in your I-CARE formulation is accountability. The 'C' is compassion. Let's think about what you might do to make sure each of these two values is reflected in your culture."

The intercom on Myerson's phone buzzed. "Excuse me for a moment." He laid down the pen, crossed over to his desk and punched the speaker phone button. Connie was on the other end of the line. "Dr. Warren is back and says he needs to speak with you right away. What should I tell him?" Myerson rested his forehead in the palm of his left hand and shook his head in disbelief then replied, "Tell Dr. Dracula that I'm planning to have lunch today in the doctor's lounge, if they'll let me in. He can see me then. Thank you Connie."

Myerson put his hands on his hips, closed his eyes, and again shook his head. Then he returned to the table. "Sorry for the interruption. Warren thinks he can interrupt me no matter what I'm doing. The man is arrogance on ice. Where were we?"

"We were about to discuss how your core value of accountability can help to shape your culture. But what I'm going to tell you is that mere accountability is not sufficient. You also need to work toward a culture of ownership. It's the difference between management and leadership. *Management* will foster a culture of accountability, while *leadership* is needed to foster a culture of ownership. And you tap into the invisible treasure of people power within your organization by moving from a culture of accountability to a culture of ownership."

Myerson rapped the table with his pen. "Well, that invisible treasure sounds great, but this is a hospital. As I told you upstairs, there do need to be rules and we do need to be accountable for those rules."

"Agreed. I'm not saying to eliminate accountability, but rather enhance it. Though based on the surveys your management team completed, it sounds like you still have work to do when it comes to holding yourselves, and each other, accountable."

"That we do," Myerson conceded.

"That's the paradox of accountability. In a culture of ownership there is more accountability, but not because you're looking over people's shoulders and holding their feet to the fire – and when you hear metaphors like 'holding your feet to the fire', is it any wonder that people tend to rebel against the notion of being held accountable? There's more accountability in a culture of ownership because people *hold themselves* accountable. Tell me, have you ever taken the trouble to wash and wax a rental car before taking the keys back to the counter?"

Myerson laughed. "No, can't say that I have."

"Nor have I, nor does anyone else. You're accountable for returning the car with a full tank of gas, so you comply, but you don't wash it or change the oil because it's not your car – there's no pride of ownership. Most organizations have lots of people who don't own their jobs, they're just renting them. Any time you hear someone say 'not my job,' or see them walk by a patient room where the call light is on, or not stoop down to pick up a piece of paper on the floor, that

> Any time someone says 'not my job,' or walks by a patient room where the call light is on, or does not pick up a piece of paper on the floor, that person is renting a space on the organization chart, not taking ownership for the work itself.

person is just renting a space on the organization chart. They're not taking ownership for the work itself."

"By that definition," Myerson said, "then yes, we have quite a few job-renters here at MMC."

"In today's world, you need leadership in every corner, not just in the corner office. And that means people need to take ownership for their work."

Myerson made a few more notes on his yellow pad. Carol Jean ate her last yellow M&M. When he'd finished writing he asked, "What are some of the ways you've helped other hospitals promote a culture of ownership?"

"We'll actually spend more time on that during the management retreat on Friday. But for now, one of my favorites is what I call the 'fill-in-the-blank job description.' I'm sure your people will come up with lots of other great ideas."

"Fill-in-the-blank job description? That sounds slightly subversive."

"Oh no, John, it's not *slightly* subversive. It's *hugely* subversive!

But it's subversive in a very positive way. And if you're not willing to tolerate – even to promote – a bit of constructive subversion, then you won't ever have leadership in every corner."

Myerson looked down at his notes, tapped the table three times with his pen, then looked back up at Carol Jean. "Well, I'm really looking forward to seeing what happens on Friday. At least I think I am."

"Oh, Friday will be a riot." John's eyes widened when Carol Jean said that, so she quickly added, "A good riot, a riot of creative thinking."

Myerson leaned back in his chair and chewed on the end of his pen. "Well, Carol Jean, I've always been a law-and-order sort of guy, but if it takes a riot to spark more creative thinking, and to promote leadership in every corner, then I guess we'll have to have a management riot." He smiled and tapped the table twice more with his pen. "Constructive subversion and management riots. Those are sort of oxymorons, aren't they?"

"Yes, and that ties into a broader paradox. Have you read the book *Leadership and the New Science* by Margaret Wheatley?"

Myerson nodded tentatively. "Yes, but quite awhile ago, so don't ask me to quote it."

"I won't, but one of the key points Wheatley made is that in organizations as in the biological world, the surest way to foster long-term stability is to have a high tolerance for short-term chaos – or at least what would appear to be chaos to the outside observer."

Myerson pursed his lips and rhythmically tapped the table with his pen. "So would that be stable chaos or chaotic stability? I'm going to have to think about that one."

"While you're thinking, shall we move on to compassion – the 'C' in I-CARE?"

"Sure. I think our people do pretty well on all five values – though we could admittedly do more to hold ourselves accountable – but I'd give us an A-plus on compassion."

"Would you now? Even though twenty-seven of twenty-nine people we passed in the hallway didn't give us so much as a see, smile and greet?"

"Okay, give us an A-minus."

Carol Jean laughed and shook her head. "Sorry, John, but you've got to finish the test before you can get your grade. In *Notes on Nursing*, Florence wrote that the most important quality in a nurse is the ability to observe – to really pay attention to the patient. To read the little cues that tell you how your patient is doing – physically, emotionally and spiritually. That's certainly the most important factor patients consider when they fill out their satisfaction surveys – were they paid attention to? And that's actually a pretty good definition for compassion: being paid attention to in an empathetic way. The ability to pay attention, and to connect emotionally, lies at the heart of being a good nurse. And, I might add, being an effective manager. Or for that matter, being a good parent. Not to mention being a happy person."

Myerson narrowed his eyes and cocked his head slightly. "I wouldn't argue with any of that. But what does it have to do with the grade we give ourselves on being compassionate?"

"Well, you can help people deal with the inner conditions that interfere with their ability to pay attention, to be present. People who are preoccupied with their own worries don't do a very good job of paying attention to others. And in today's world, there's one worry that is pretty much omnipresent. It's a worry that keeps caregivers from connecting with their patients, managers from connecting with their people, and parents from connecting with their children. It's…"

Myerson laughed as he interrupted. "Don't tell me – it's invisible!"

Carol Jean's cheeks tinged red. "Well, yes. Worry is invisible. But no less real for the fact. And let's get to the one that's probably at the top of the list in today's world. Do you know the average credit card debt being carried by your employees?"

"No I don't. But what's that got to do with compassion? And why's it my business?"

"Nine-thousand, five-hundred dollars. That's the national average, and I doubt your people vary from that average by much. That is above and beyond their mortgage, car payments, school loans and other debts. And it's your business because every time one of your people worries about those debts, they're not going to be fully engaged in their work. It's an invisible drain on patient care quality, on productivity, and on teamwork."

"You know, Carol Jean, these people are grown-ups. I can't follow them around slapping their hands every time they pull out their credit cards. There has to be an element of personal responsibility." Myerson absent-mindedly looked at his watch, a signal that anyone on his staff would have known meant it was time to move on to a different topic.

Carol Jean ignored the signal. "Of course you can't follow people around watching how they spend their money. And of course there has to be personal responsibility. But you *could* sponsor classes on how to manage money – something many of your people have probably never been taught. You *could* set up a debtors anonymous support group under hospital sponsorship. You *could* retain a personal finance coach to help people hold themselves accountable for more effectively managing their money."

Myerson put his elbow on the arm of the chair, rested his chin across his thumb with his forefinger hooked over his nose, and furrowed his brow at Carol Jean. Then he looked at his watch again. She pressed on. "One of Nightingale's biographers referred to the 'love affair' between the ordinary British soldier and their lady with the lamp. One reason they loved her so well is that she didn't only tend to their clinical needs, she also helped them take care of their personal needs, including their money. Back then soldiers had no way to safely send their pay back to England, and in Turkey there was nothing to spend it on but booze, so they drank it away. Nightingale took it upon herself to help them repatriate their paychecks. Then she set up a library so they'd have something to do with their time. And guess what? To the eternal astonishment of the British brass who – like Wellington before them – thought of their soldiers as the 'scum of the earth,' a lot of them actually sobered up and started to read."

Myerson's finger remained hooked over the top of his nose, but his frown softened. Carol Jean continued. "In today's terms, Nightingale created a win-win. The soldiers were healthier, their families got taken care of, and the generals got a better fighting force. And when it comes to the biggest challenge you are going to face in the years to come – recruiting and retaining good people – something like this can make two really good things happen."

They sat in silence for a moment. Myerson finally said, "Okay, what two things?"

"Well, first and most obvious, some of your people might actually take you up on your offer of help. They might start to get their finances under better control. This will not only make them more productive and enthusiastic on the job, it will make their home lives happier as well. Are you aware that financial problems are a leading cause of divorce?"

"I'd heard that. And the second benefit?"

"If you can help someone wipe out a nine-thousand dollar credit card debt, don't you think they'd be less likely to move across town for a twenty-cent pay raise?" Just that morning, Saint John's Hospital had announced a new pay scale for support staff that was, in fact, about twenty cents an hour more than Memorial's current starting rate.

Myerson again rapped the table with his pen, then made a note on one of the cards he always carried in his shirt pocket. "Alright, we'll look into it."

"Good. Helping people deal with personal problems like debt is often the first step to cutting loose the invisible anchor that's putting a drag on every dimension of your organization's performance."

Myerson quickly looked to his left and his right, then up to the ceiling and down to the floor. "You must have terribly good eyesight, Carol Jean, to keep seeing all of these things that are invisible to everyone else."

Carol Jean laughed. "John, if you only knew. Let me explain what I mean by the invisible anchor. If two teams of equally talented, trained, and coached players are competing with the only difference being that players on one team all have positive self-images and high self-esteem, while players on the other team have poor self-images and low self-esteem, who would you bet on to win the game?"

"Is this a trick question?"

"No, not at all. And you know the answer. A winning team is built around individual team members who know how to think and act like winning players. And those are learnable skills. I hear you and your leadership team talk about teamwork, about having a winning team, but I see little evidence that you're doing much to invest in helping every person in your organization see themselves as winners in the game of life. Quite to the contrary, I know some of your executive team – people who should know better – think it's all a bunch of new age, touchy-feely hogwash." Carol Jean looked at Myerson over the top of her reading glasses. "Am I right?"

Myerson sat in stony silence.

"In fact," Carol Jean went on, "haven't you said as much yourself?"

Myerson finally smiled and shrugged. "Yes, but that was back in the old days, before you enlightened me."

> Once a critical mass of people makes the commitment to their personal transformation, it will inevitably have a positive transformative impact on the entire organization.

"Glad to do it," Carol Jean replied with a smile of her own. "But seriously, if we're really going to work on the invisible architecture of this organization, it follows that we should help your people work on their own inner architecture as well, since it takes winning players to build a winning team. Some people won't want to take us up on the offer of helping them change their lives for the better. Some will say it's a bunch of touchy-feely new age hogwash, and some will even make fun of others who are trying to improve their lives. That's to be expected – but not necessarily to be tolerated."

Myerson's door opened and Connie stepped partway in. "Just a reminder, John – your conference call is in ten minutes."

"I'll wrap up and let you get ready for your call," Carol Jean said. "When we meet with your executive team, I'll say more about this, but it's an essential element in moving from a culture of accountability toward a culture of ownership. Once you have a critical mass of individuals making that commitment to personal transformation, it cannot help but have a positive transformative impact on the entire organization."

They stood and shook hands. "This doesn't sound like a quick fix," said Myerson.

"Afraid not."

"Don't you have some sort of PowerPoint presentation we can make everyone sit through and then get on with our business?"

"Believe me, John, I wish it were that simple. But if you and your team make this investment now, you'll reap the rewards for a long time to come. This *is* your business."

On her way out, Carol Jean stopped to thank Connie again, and to liberate four brown M&Ms from the candy jar on her desk. She had an hour before her next meeting. Munching on M&Ms as she walked, Carol Jean went out to the healing garden in the hospital courtyard. Florence Nightingale was waiting for her on one of the benches. "That went quite well, don't you think?" Nightingale said as Carol Jean sat down next to her.

"Yes, I think so. If John Myerson and his team can't cultivate a culture of ownership here at MMC, I'm not sure it can be done anywhere. I like him a lot. He asks good questions, and he really listens."

"Two essential attributes of leadership. In my career I asked lots of good questions, but probably could have done a better job of listening." Nightingale smiled at the sight of a little girl stretching out on tiptoes so she could dip her fingers into the water of the fountain. "There are a lot of good people in this hospital," she said. "In every hospital, I'll warrant. You need to reach the leaders among them, the ones who can influence the others. Leaders like Sarah Rutledge. Bring people like her along and most of the rest will follow."

"I hope you're right," Carol Jean replied, "but I've sure got my work cut out for me." Carol Jean had hardly blinked, but as those last words were coming out of her mouth, she realized she was talking to thin air. Nightingale had disappeared.

"Hey lady, are you homeless?" The little girl from the fountain was now at Carol Jean's feet, with wide-eyed curiosity and a gap-toothed smile. She couldn't have been more than five. Carol Jean smiled and bent toward her. "No, I'm not homeless. Why would you think that?" Carol Jean looked up from the little girl and saw her mother standing over by the fountain, just watching. She recognized her as one of the nurses she'd seen while being given a tour of the emergency department.

"My mommy says homeless people have invisible friends they talk to. Were you talking to an invisible friend? Mommy says invisible friends are just make-believe, but I think they're real."

If you only knew, Carol Jean thought to herself. "Well, your mommy is right – most of the time. But there are some invisible friends," Carol Jean leaned closer to the little girl and whispered, "who are only real to the people who see them. Aren't there?" The little girl nodded emphatically, her pigtails bobbing up and down. "But we keep those invisible friends secret, just to ourselves, don't we?"

The little girl nodded again, more solemnly this time. "If you're homeless, you can come home with me," she said with the earnestness of a child who has yet to learn distrust. "And we can play with our invisible friends."

Carol Jean smiled at the memories of her daughters, and now her granddaughters, and the invisible friends they'd all made, each in their own time. She'd always considered invisible friends to be a special gift, and never more so than the day over a year ago that Florence Nightingale stood by her side at Waterloo Place in London wanting to know what had changed, and what more needed to change, in our hospitals. "I'd love to go home with you to play with our invisible friends, little girl, but I have to go to a meeting with a doctor in a few minutes."

"Are you sick?" The little girl's face conveyed a genuine depth of concern.

"No, I'm not sick. Part of my job is to talk with doctors."

"My brother is sick," said the little girl, shrugging her shoulders and looking down at the Mary Janes on her feet. "But mommy says he's going to get better."

"I'm sure he will. They have very good doctors here. What's your brother's name?"

"Timmy," said the little girl, instantly lighting up at the sound of her brother's name.

"Well, I'm sure Timmy is a wonderful big brother."

"Yeth he is," she lisped through the space between her two front teeth.

Carol Jean leaned farther forward. "Well, you tell Timmy and your invisible friends hello from me and my invisible friend, okay?

"What's her name?"

"My invisible friend? Her name is Florence. I'll tell her you said hello, okay?"

"Okay!" the little girl squealed with a wild smile that made Carol Jean want to pick her up and hold her, then ran laughing back to her mother.

CHAPTER EIGHT

"I have to tell you, Carol Jean, I've been at this hospital for nearly 30 years and I've seen consultants come and go, taking their programs with them. Every new CEO wants to put a mark on the organization with the help of some consultant. We've been magnetized and harmonized, Disneyfied and culturized. We've been hardwired and wirelessed, six sigmafied and desiloized, we've been leaned and we've been meaned. And you know what? The more things change, the more they stay the same. So you'll have to forgive this old country doctor if I seem a bit skeptical about this latest and greatest new program of the month."

Charlie Franklin was an orthopedic surgeon who had also recently been elected president of the medical staff. He had a reputation for being hard-working and tough-minded. And for being always truthful and rarely tactful. Carol Jean thought back to the reception Florence Nightingale had received from the doctors at Scutari, who'd told her in no uncertain terms they wanted nothing to do with her band of nurses and their "program," and wondered if Dr. Franklin was somehow communing with those physicians the way she'd been communing with Florence.

"Actually, Dr. Franklin, I totally agree that the last thing you need is another program of the month. That's certainly not something I'm here to do. However, I'll bet if you really think about it, these 'programs' have had a cumulative impact. I mean, a lot of good things have happened here over the past several years; don't you think these so-called programs deserve at least some of the credit?"

Dr. Franklin nodded grudgingly. "Perhaps. So, tell me about The Florence Prescription. Just what are you prescribing for us?"

"Well," Carol Jean replied, "there are really two parts to that answer, though they are related."

"Consultants' answers always come in two or more parts," Dr. Franklin said with a wry smile.

"Wouldn't you be suspicious if I had one easy answer for your complex problems?"

Franklin narrowed his eyes, focusing his gaze even more intently on Carol Jean, then nodded – a little less grudgingly this time. "Go on."

"The first part of the answer is that we'll be working with the hospital leadership team on what I call the 'invisible architecture' of your organization. Think about this: from the time I pull into the parking lot of Memorial Medical Center, my first impressions are primarily created by your physical facilities. But if I'm a patient in bed for three or four days, or a staff nurse who's considering a job offer from somewhere else, that visible architecture won't play any part in my thinking, will it?" Almost imperceptibly, Franklin shook his head no. "What determines how I perceive the quality of my experience as a patient, or whether the hospital has earned my loyalty as an employee, will be determined by my feelings, and how I feel is determined by your invisible architecture."

"You're going to have to tell me a bit more about this invisible architecture notion of yours."

"Certainly. Winston Churchill once said that we shape our buildings, and then our buildings shape us. But as patients and as employees, our attitudes, beliefs and behaviors are not shaped by the buildings as much as they are by the values, the culture, and the emotional climate of our

> Our attitudes, beliefs and behaviors are influenced by the values, culture, and emotional climate of our organization. These are the key elements of invisible architecture.

organization. These are the three key elements of invisible architecture. They build one upon the other as surely as the visible walls rest upon the underlying foundation of a visible structure. The problem is that we put little or no thought into – if I may stretch the metaphor – the design and construction of that invisible architecture."

"For obvious reasons, it seems to me," Dr. Franklin said, leaning back and shoving his hands deep into the pockets of his long white lab coat. "How do you design, much less build, something you can't see?"

"Fair question," Carol Jean replied. "Let's look at another analogy. In Florence Nightingale's day there was a raging debate about what caused diseases like tuberculosis and dysentery to be spread. Do you recall the reason there was so much resistance by doctors to washing their hands?"

Franklin not only smiled, he actually chuckled (something very few people ever saw him do). "Because germs are invisible, and doctors couldn't believe their hands were crawling with the little buggers."

"Fortunately, we've got that one solved, don't we?" Carol Jean mimicked washing her hands. "There is one hundred percent compliance with the hand-washing protocols here at Memorial, right?" Franklin chuckled again but didn't need to say anything, because they both knew that – more than a century and a half after the time of Florence Nightingale and the public health pioneers of her generation – compliance was still far short of perfection at MMC and almost every other hospital in the country.

"We can draw up gorgeous blueprints for the visible architecture of Memorial Medical Center," Carol Jean continued. "The management team can go on retreats and conceptualize brilliant strategic plans. We can make everyone go through customer service training, and we can put billboards up on the highway telling everyone how caring and compassionate we are. But unless people change how they think and act, all we'll have is a pretty picture of an organization that exists only in our dreams. That's the second part of the answer. And by far the most difficult. To make the picture real, people have to buy-in, to take ownership. That means they need to change their attitudes and their behaviors. They need to change the way they treat each other. And in my experience, one group that is in greatest need of making those changes is also the group that tends to be most resistant to making them."

"You are referring, I presume, to the medical staff."

"Yes I am. Here's the problem: like every other hospital, Memorial Medical Center is hierarchical and status-conscious. If we really want people to feel a sense of ownership for MMC, we need to bring down the status barriers."

"You mean make all the doctors drive Chevys instead of Volvos?"

"No, I'm talking about much more simple things. Like the way people treat each other in the corridors and on patient care units, or in the operating room. Really, I'm speaking of nothing less than a revolution in which we treat people as people, not just as job descriptions with legs. I've spoken with John Myerson about putting together a task force on dignity. We're not sure that's what we'll call it, but that's what it's for – simple dignity."

Franklin sighed heavily. "You know, it's beyond me the way you consultants can come into a place, sniff around a bit, and think you know all our problems, and the solutions to those problems, better than we know them. Astonishing, really."

Carol Jean didn't know how to respond. *He really is of a kind with Dr. Menzies, Nightingale's chief antagonist at Scutari,* she thought to herself.

"Oh no, my dear, compared to that awful man Dr. Menzies, Dr. Franklin here is a lovable puppy dog, no matter how gruff he attempts to appear on the outside." It was the voice of Florence Nightingale, who had just materialized in the chair next to Carol Jean. "I think you'll find that when good Dr. Franklin realizes there really is a problem, he will become your most ardent ally."

Franklin pushed back so hard in his chair that he almost fell over backwards, closed his eyes and vigorously shook his head, then appeared to be both shocked and angry when Nightingale was still sitting in his office after the attempt to clear his head of the figment had failed.

"Dr. Franklin, meet Florence Nightingale," said Carol Jean as she looked from one to the other. It took a lot to rattle Charlie Franklin, the former combat surgeon who was known for being steady as a giant redwood in a storm, no matter what crisis might happen to occur in the operating room. But seeing Florence Nightingale suddenly appear in his office rattled him. Nightingale tipped her head in his direction and with a mischievous smile said, "It's a pleasure to meet you, Dr. Franklin. And I'm looking forward to having you be a part of our little conspiracy."

"Conspiracy?" Franklin looked up to the corner of the room as if in hopes of finding that a holographic projector had been installed in his office without his knowledge.

"Yes, conspiracy," Nightingale said. "Carol Jean has been talking about the invisible architecture of the hospital... Oh dear!" she exclaimed, looking back at Carol Jean with another laugh. "I just don't believe I'll *ever* be able to think of a place of healing as a medical center rather than a hospital!" Returning her attention to Dr. Franklin she said, "The whole effort of changing your invisible architecture must begin with the commitment that people will treat each other with mutual respect and dignity. At Scutari, the British officers all wanted their own private nurses, the best food, and the most comfortable quarters – and soldiers took the hindmost. I made many enemies by my insistence that we would tend to our soldiers based upon their medical needs and not their rank, religion or social standing. It took a long time, but we finally did change the culture of the British military system. That in turn had an egalitarian effect on the society at large. Even so far as to begin a social transformation of the caste system in far-off India, in those days a British colony. Here too, it's going to take the quiet collaboration of prominent people at all levels insisting upon changes in how we treat each other, beginning with their own examples. A conspiracy for dignity, if you will."

"With all due respect, Miss Nightingale," Franklin said, still not sure if he was speaking to a holographic projection, a figment of his imagination, or if there had just been a tremor in the cosmos, "this is not India. The idea that all men, and women, are created equal is not just a commendable notion, it's been part of our heritage since 1776. There is no caste system in America, or in our medical center."

"Ah, yes, 1776," Nightingale replied. "The year King George lost the colonies. But there *is* a caste system in your country, and in your hospital, Dr. Franklin. Your caste system is much more subtle, but it is every bit as real as was the caste system in India. You do not, of course, use the terms Brahman and Untouchable, but the distinctions are very clear. White lab coat people in the surgery suite and blue suit people in the executive suite are your Brahmans, and work shirt people down in housekeeping and food service are your Untouchables."

Franklin shook his head. "That might be the case in other hospitals, but here at Memorial everybody gets treated pretty much the same no matter what their job title happens to be."

"Is that a fact?"

"Yes it is. As Carol Jean knows, I've been here a long time and I can assure you that we treat each other like family."

Nightingale pursed her lips and nodded. Only Carol Jean noticed how the hands folded in her lap clenched more tightly upon each other. "Since you are so sure of yourself, Dr. Franklin, are you willing to put this to an empirical test?"

"I'm not certain how you would go about empirically testing the hypothesis, Miss Nightingale, but if you can find a way, sure, I'll go along with a test."

"Oh, there absolutely is a way, but you will need to leave this office."

"Okay, I'm ready." Dr. Franklin started to rise from his chair. "Let's go."

Nightingale winked at Carol Jean. "Actually, Dr. Franklin, we won't be going with you. You'll be making this trip on your own."

In less time than it took for the left ventricle of his heart to contract, Charlie Franklin found himself standing at the busiest intersection of Memorial Medical Center with a mop in his hands and the brown shirt of an MMC housekeeper on his back. At the spot right in front of his feet someone had recently thrown up, a fact obvious to any nose within 30 feet of the mess. Franklin recoiled and puckered his face. Looking up, he saw his friend Will Jordan, Memorial's chief of medicine, coming down the corridor engrossed in animated discussion with a group of medical students. Franklin shrugged and smiled self-consciously.

Dr. Jordan looked at Dr. Franklin with the sort of regard one might give a cockroach found nesting in a tennis shoe, then without saying a word marched right by, not missing a beat in his pontification to the medical students.

"What's *your* problem?" Franklin muttered under his breath. From the other direction, a woman walked by with her adolescent son. With a surreptitious nod in Franklin's direction she said, "*That's* why you need to go to college, Marcus, so you don't end up doing *that* for a living." Marcus looked at the mess on the floor, looked at Franklin, and made a face. Franklin realized that he had been the object of this mother's little motivational lecture and her son's scorn.

Standing there with his mop in his hand, Franklin began to feel like the invisible man. Everyone gave him a wide berth and looked the other way as they passed by. He turned to look through the glass window out into the courtyard. In the exact spot where he should have seen his own reflection looking back at him, Franklin instead saw the reflection of a young man of obvious Hispanic heritage holding a mop in his hands. He squinted at the backwards reflection of the letters embroidered above the man's shirt pocket: Carlos. Franklin lifted the mop eight inches off the ground. So did Carlos. Staring at the reflection in the glass, he lifted one leg. So did Carlos. He held his left arm out to the side. So did Carlos. Mimicking something he'd once seen in a movie, he held the mop as if it were a dancing partner and did a bit of a waltz. So did Carlos. "So this is Nightingale's empirical test," he muttered to himself.

"And just what do you think you're doing, Carlos?" Franklin took his eyes off the dancing reflection in the window and saw Margaret Munoz glaring up at him, fists planted firmly on her hips. He didn't know her personally, but had always heard good things about the housekeeping supervisor. "Do you think this mess is going to clean itself up while you dance with your mop?" Munoz sniffed and puffed her chest in supervisory self-importance. "You know, Carlos, there's a lot of people looking for jobs out there. If you don't want to work,

I'll find someone who does. Then you can dance with your mop all day." Munoz looked over at her reflection in the window, puffed a little more, and glared back at Franklin. "Now clean this mess up. And you can be sure I'll be coming back to check up on you."

Franklin watched Munoz go steaming down the corridor like a submarine-hunter on a search-and-destroy mission. Then he looked down at the puddle of puke on the floor. Dr. Charlie Franklin routinely sliced into human skin and sawed through human bones, and he knew his way around the autopsy suite as well as he did his own bedroom. But pushing his mop into the mess on the floor in front of him caused him to gag like a first year medical student cutting into his first corpse. He felt light-headed and struggled to catch his breath as his heart raced into overdrive.

As he stood there struggling to regain both physical and emotional balance, Franklin felt a tug on his sleeve. Looking down, he saw a little boy in a hospital gown holding onto an IV pole that towered above him. He recognized the boy as Timmy Mallory, the son of an MMC emergency department nurse. In the doctors' lounge the other day, he'd overheard two of the oncologists discussing the boy's case. "Not good," Dr. Hayes had said with a sad shake of the head. But there was no hint of that prognosis in Timmy's big smile. "Hi Carlos," Timmy said, "I'm sorry I made this mess and you have to clean it up. Want me to help?"

Franklin shook his head. "That's alright. I can take care of it."

Timmy stood up on his tiptoes and pulled harder on Franklin's sleeve. Franklin saw an earnestness in the boy's eyes which, it occurred to him, one tended to grow out of long before graduating from medical school. "Did the lady talk to you, Carlos? The lady with the lamp? Are you going to help us?"

Before he could answer, Franklin was back in his office facing Carol Jean Hawtrey and Florence Nightingale. "So, Dr. Franklin," Nightingale innocently asked, "what were the results of our little test? How did it feel to be 'just' a housekeeper?" Looking at Carol Jean she said, "It's ironic, don't you think, that used in that fashion 'just' is the most unjust word in the English language?" Looking back to Franklin she asked, "What shall we tell little Timmy?"

Franklin ignored her question and looked directly at Carol Jean. "This committee on dignity you mentioned; do you have someone to chair it yet?" Carol Jean shook her head no. "You do now," he said with a look of iron-willed determination that was usually hidden behind a mask in the operating room.

❖ ❖ ❖

It was 7:30 in the evening and since leaving Dr. Franklin's office, Carol Jean had been on her feet almost the entire day as department directors gave her tours of their areas. She envied the joggers in their comfortable running shoes as she walked the three blocks from the hospital to the city park. This evening she had to prepare for a half-day session with the nursing leadership team scheduled for the next morning, but first she wanted to clear her mind, and hopefully get a shot of much-needed energy and inspiration.

Florence Nightingale was standing by the pond watching a flotilla of ducks making its way toward a group of children all clutching bags full of breadcrumbs. Carol Jean sat down on the bench, kicked off her high heels and wiggled her toes. By now she was learning it was not wise, when in a public place, to be too obvious about carrying on a conversation with someone that no one else could see. At length, Nightingale came over and sat on the bench next to her. "How was the day, CJ?"

> What any of us call our own era depends upon what we choose to see – the best of times or the worst of times. And what we choose to see today – and how leaders choose to frame reality when speaking with their people – will profoundly shape the future they create. Perspective shapes reality.

Carol Jean arched one eyebrow. Nobody outside of her immediate family ever called her CJ. "I don't know how you did it, Flo" Carol Jean replied, deciding she would reciprocate the familiarity by using Nightingale's family nickname. "I doubt I walked anywhere close to the distance you covered at Scutari, and still my feet are killing me."

"Are they now?"

"Well, they're not *really* killing me, it just feels like it."

"Be careful the words you use," Nightingale said. "I've always believed that the mind can affect the body, that words can have a healing – or destroying – power. You really do, you know, live in the golden age of healthcare."

"I suppose so," Carol Jean replied, "but I don't think everyone sees it that way. Listening to some of the people at the hospitals I work with, you'd think the golden age of healthcare came and went a long time ago."

Nightingale looked wistfully at the children feeding the ducks. "In my day there was a writer popular in London. Charles Dickens. Have you heard of him?"

"Of course. He's actually quite famous now. His Christmas Carol story – the one with Scrooge and the three ghosts of Christmas – got made into a movie."

"Movie?"

"Yeah." Carol Jean started to explain motion pictures, then decided that not only would it take to long, Nightingale almost certainly wouldn't have been interested in the ways people entertained themselves today. Instead she settled for saying, "Think of it as a way to watch a book being acted out, usually in a very abbreviated way."

Nightingale stared blankly. "Abbreviated? Why would anyone want to abbreviate a great book?"

Carol Jean just shrugged.

Nightingale continued, "Dickens began his tale of the French Revolution with this line: It was the best of times, it was the worst of times."

"Yes!" Carol Jean exclaimed. "*A Tale of Two Cities!*"

"You read the book?"

"I saw the movie."

"Oh. I see. Well, that line defines the state of healthcare in every age. In my time, in your time, and in any future time. It was, is, and will be the best of times; it was, is, and will be the worst of times.

What any of us call our own era depends upon what we choose to see – the best of times or the worst of times. And what we choose to see today – and how leaders choose to frame reality when speaking with their people – will profoundly shape the future they create. You know it as the Pygmalion effect, or as the placebo effect. The law of the self-fulfilling prophecy. Perspective shapes reality.

CHAPTER NINE

Linda Martinez was the newest member of the MMC leadership team. She'd joined just over a year ago as Executive Vice President and Chief Nursing Officer. She was new to the organization, but she and Myerson had a long relationship. She'd been director of nursing at Presbyterian Hospital when Myerson was first COO, then CEO of that organization. "Linda is a master of gentle pressure relentlessly applied," Myerson had told Carol Jean. "She could whittle down a mountaintop with a feather if she had enough time." He'd gone on to say that she was a powerful advocate for patient-centered care. "It's a bigger transition than most people appreciate; MMC has always been very process- and procedure-centered, with patients being force-fit into the model. Linda is turning that paradigm upside down."

Carol Jean had yet to meet Martinez in person because she and several other members of the nursing leadership team spent the first part of the week visiting Griffin Hospital in Connecticut to learn more about the Planetree approach to patient-centered care. But they'd become friends through long-distance correspondence, and Carol Jean owed Martinez a huge debt of gratitude. Several years previously, Martinez had written an editorial in the *American Journal of Nursing* praising *Leadership Lessons from Florence Nightingale*. Within a month, the publisher ran a second printing of Carol Jean's book that was ten times larger than the first. Today, they'd planned a brief private meeting after which they would join the rest of the nursing leadership team for an offsite retreat. They'd agreed upon *Empowering Patients Begins with Empowered Caregivers* as the topic.

Carol Jean pulled into the parking lot fifteen minutes early for their 7 a.m. meeting, and Martinez was waiting for her in the hospital lobby. "It's wonderful to finally meet you in person," Carol Jean said as they embraced like old friends. She followed Martinez back to her office in the executive suite. When they'd settled in at the small conference table, Carol Jean with a cup of coffee and Martinez with herb tea, Carol Jean opened her briefcase and extracted a gift-wrapped box. "In appreciation for all you've done for me – and for Florence," she said as she pushed the gift across the table.

Martinez picked up the box and tipped it from side-to-side, like a child trying to guess what's wrapped inside a Christmas present. "You really didn't need to do this, Carol Jean. I enjoyed your book, and I think every caregiver – and we are *all* caregivers – should read it. So that's what I said in my AJN editorial." She set the box back down on the table. It was the size of a loaf of bread. "Can I open it?"

"Absolutely! I hope you like it."

Martinez pulled the ribbon, tore off the wrapping paper and opened the top of the box. "Oh, it's beautiful!" she exclaimed as she pulled an elongated brown cylinder from the box. It looked like an accordion made of weathered leather stood on end, with a brass handle at the top and a polished wood base at the bottom. "What is it?"

"It's a replica of the Turkish lamp that Florence Nightingale – the lady with the lamp – used for her midnight rounds through the Scutari Barrack Hospital. I thought it would be a great metaphor for our work together: lighting the way for organizational transformation, moving forward by remembering the legacy of our past."

"I love it!" Martinez admired the lamp, then noticed the inscription engraved on a brass plaque at the base:

PROCEED UNTIL APPREHENDED

"It's perfect, Carol Jean. Thank you! *Proceed until apprehended* really captures the empowered spirit I want to promote. When it comes to doing the right thing for our patients, and for each other, don't sit around waiting for instructions or permission – proceed until apprehended." Martinez set the lamp down on the table with an approving nod. "It's beautiful," she said again.

"It was also very functional in its day." Florence Nightingale stood at the table, hands folded in front of her, and leaned over to inspect the lamp. "Remarkable," she said. "A perfect verisimilitude." As Martinez gaped in amazement, Nightingale settled into the third chair, rested her chin on interlaced fingers and serenely gazed into the lamp and the memories it held for her. At last she said, "The way your hospitals are all lit up, day and night, is certainly more practical than the lamp I used for making my rounds, but I do miss the shadows."

Knowing Myerson's penchant for pulling practical jokes, Martinez had just laughed when he'd warned her that Florence Nightingale herself might pop in unannounced. Now she laughed again, but a much more nervous sort of laughter. She checked to see that the door to her office was still closed (it was) then to see if Nightingale was still sitting there at the table (she was).

"It's a pleasure to meet you, Mrs. Martinez," Nightingale said with a warm smile and a slight bow of the head. "I've heard wonderful things about what you are doing here, from both Carol Jean and John Myerson."

Martinez blinked hard and shook her head. "So it really is true. The lady with the lamp has come to pay us a visit here at Memorial. I believe my eyes right now, but I'm not sure I'll believe my memory tomorrow."

"People vastly overrate the accuracy of their memories," Nightingale said, "while they vastly underrate the power of their vision. So what you remember about our meeting today means a lot less than what you decide to do as a result."

For the tiniest fragment of time, Linda Martinez had a vivid impression of Florence Nightingale gliding through the halls of the Scutari Barrack Hospital. It was so real that she felt as if she herself was walking alongside the lady with the lamp. She could hear the moans of men drifting through the nightmares of their final hours, could see their vague forms haunting shadows that were barely illuminated by Nightingale's lamp, could smell their broken bodies and sense the ever-so tentative hold with which those bodies still clung to their souls. Then, just as suddenly, she was back in her office at Memorial Medical Center. She closed her eyes, trying to recreate the experience, but it was already fading into the netherworld of imagination.

Nightingale gazed into the lamp as she spoke. "I always thought of them as my children, those poor British soldiers sent to die for no good reason in a war that did not need to be. There was nothing I wouldn't do for them, even when I knew that all I could do would not be enough. Especially then."

"Perhaps the defining paradox of Florence Nightingale," Carol Jean said, "is that she was a deeply emotional person who knew when she had to set her emotions aside. She was the very picture of compassion – the lady with the lamp who first defined what patient-centered care really means. And at the same time, she was a tough-minded manager for whom operational efficiency was a prerequisite for compassionate care. Did you know that Florence was the very first person to calculate the cost per patient day in a healthcare organization?"

> Empowerment isn't something that can be given; it's a choice that must be made. No one can empower you but you, and once you've given yourself that power no one can take it away from you.

Nightingale smiled at the recollection. "I was quite proud of that, actually. At Harley Street – the facility I managed before being called to Turkey – we reduced our cost per patient day from one shilling and ten pence to one shilling and a halfpenny."

"In our retreat later this morning," Carol Jean said, "we're going to be talking about empowerment. But empowerment isn't something that can be given; it's a choice that must be made. No one can empower you but you, and once you've given yourself that power no one can take it away from you. If you can give someone empowerment, you can also take it away, and loaned empowerment isn't the real thing. Furthermore, you can't empower someone who doesn't already have that sense of self-empowerment. It's like trying to push water up a hill. Can't be done. Florence had an influence that was far out of proportion to the authority of her official position because rather than wait for someone else to empower her, she decided and she acted."

"To see what is right and not to do it is cowardice," Nightingale said with a grave nod. "Confucius said that. It takes courage to be empowered."

Martinez ran her finger across the brass plaque on the base of the lamp. *Proceed Until Apprehended.* "You know, we really do have a great staff here at Memorial. Most of them want to do the right thing, but I think there's a real fear that they'll be apprehended – which I guess happened quite a bit under the previous administration. So a part of our challenge will be helping people to unlearn those old responses because we are in a new world." Looking over at Carol Jean she said, "I think *The Self-Empowerment Pledge* will give us a great start."

Carol Jean nodded. "I've seen some amazing – even miraculous – things happen when people take those seven simple promises to heart and act upon them."

"Will you be joining us for the…" Before Martinez could finish her question, the chair in which Nightingale had been sitting was vacant. Looking back at Carol Jean and laughing she said, "I hate to admit it, but as I was sitting here listening to the most famous nurse in the history of our profession, I kept wondering how I could possibly explain – her – to my nursing leadership team. Pretty funny, huh?"

Carol Jean smiled sympathetically. "I understand. Believe me, I completely understand. But I don't think we need to worry about

Florence showing up at our retreat. She was planning to spend some time with her brave little soldier."

"Her soldier?"

"I'll explain later. In fact, I'll introduce you. But for now," she said, looking at her watch, "we had better get going. It's not a good thing to show up late for your own retreat."

❖ ❖ ❖

It wasn't unusual for Timmy – who of late had taken on the name Sir Timothy, Dragonslayer – to speak with people and creatures unseen by others, so nobody who passed by his room that afternoon took notice of the fact that he appeared to be engaged in an animated discussion with the air. Only he could see Florence Nightingale sitting on his bedside; only he could hear her side of the conversation.

"The dragons came back last night," Timmy said in a voice of bottomless sadness. Nightingale took his right hand, his sword-wielding hand, in both of hers but said nothing. "There were too many." His lower lip quivered and he fought back tears, trying to be the brave little soldier Florence Nightingale believed him to be. "I tried to fight, but there were so many of them, breathing fire on me, biting at me with bloody fangs." As he sank back into nightmares of the previous night, Timmy's last defense against despair crumbled and he cried. "In my nightmare," he wailed, "the dragons killed Sir Timothy, Miss Nightingale. Does that mean that now I have to die?"

Nightingale put a hand against Timmy's check, hot with fever and wet with tears. "No, Timmy. Every army loses battles before it wins the war. You have lost a battle, but you must not lose hope and courage. There are many more battles to come, and you must be strong."

Timmy's call light had been on for the past half hour. Nightingale watched as people scurried past, oblivious to the little light above the door and the frightened little boy inside the room. Nurses hurrying along on their rounds, the housekeeper buffing the floor, a woman from the medical records department pushing a cart piled with charts, a pair of doctors talking about a patient on another unit. Not one person even looked in the door of Timmy's room, or even seemed to notice that his call light was lit.

"We can do better than this," Florence Nightingale muttered to herself. "We must do better than this."

CHAPTER TEN

The first thing MMC's nurse managers saw when they entered the Pine Ridge Room of the Marriott Conference Center was a banner stretched across the north wall that read:

99,280 Promises To Change Our World

When they asked either Linda or Carol Jean what it meant, they were simply told they'd have to wait to find out. At each of the 68 place settings was a sealed 9" x 12" envelope with the word *I'm-Powered* printed on the outside in big block letters. At precisely 9:00, Martinez strode to the front of the room, pleased to note that every place setting was already occupied by a member of her management team. When she'd arrived two years earlier, she'd struck a bargain with the nurse managers. She'd expect them to show up for scheduled meetings on time and ready to get to work, and in return she wouldn't waste their time with unnecessary, or unnecessarily prolonged, meetings. It had taken a while for people to realize she was serious on both counts, but now her meetings started on time and ended early, with very little wasted motion in between.

Martinez launched right into her subject. "You all remember that last year we had a rash of patient complaints about lost items – false teeth, glasses, books, cell phones, and even an iPod or two. It was taking the risk management people over a week to conclude their investigations. In every single case, the item not being found, we ended up paying for a replacement – but usually not until after the patient had gone home – and gone home pretty hungry if it was a pair of false teeth we lost. As you recall, we made the decision to empower our floor nurses to commit the hospital to replacing such items on the spot. We put an upper limit of five hundred dollars, so risk management still gets involved with lost diamond rings or sports cars." This remark was greeted with a round of laughter; they'd all heard about the man who tried to get the hospital to reimburse him for a Porsche he'd claimed had been stolen from the parking ramp with his wife's diamond ring in the glove compartment.

"As I recall, the biggest concern we had was that some nurses might go overboard and commit the hospital to compensating people for things they hadn't really lost. Well, folks, the numbers are in." Martinez pulled a sheet of paper from her suit coat pocket and unfolded it. "Over the past twelve months, risk management has received twenty-three claims for lost items. The number of those for which one of our floor nurses had already committed us to make a replacement?" Martinez surveyed the room, her eyes inviting someone to make a guess. No one did, so she continued. "Precisely zero." She let that sink in for a moment. "For all of our talk about empowering people, somehow that power never made it to the front lines."

A look of dismay came over the audience, with a few even burying their faces in their hands as they shook their heads. "It's not your fault," Martinez insisted. "I now realize my mistake. We've been trying to empower our people without first teaching them what it means to be empowered, and how to go about empowering themselves." Martinez signaled for Carol Jean to join her at the front of the room. "I know many of you have read Carol Jean Hawtrey's book on what we can learn about leadership from the life and work of Florence Nightingale. Today it's our privilege to have her join us to share a prescription for personal empowerment."

Carol Jean acknowledged the polite applause then asked everyone to open their envelopes. "The word on the cover is not a typo," she said. "It's intended to convey the fact that a manager cannot *empower* anyone who does not already consider him or herself to be empowered. Or, as I've put it on your envelopes, to be *I'm-Powered*. Before we start, though, let's do a little survey. There are two three-by-five cards in your envelopes. Please pull them out." As people extracted the cards, Carol Jean gave one of the nurse managers in the front row a calculator and asked her to be the official statistician for the coming exercise. "On the blue card, I want you to rate the MMC culture on a scale of one-to-five for how empowering it is, with one being that Attila the Hun would be right at home here, and five being that the MMC philosophy is that it's better to ask forgiveness than permission." When everyone had completed their cards, Carol Jean had them all passed to the front and asked her appointed statistician to calculate an average.

"Okay now, on the green card," Carol Jean said, "please rate your own behavior on a one-to-five scale, with one being that you hide out like Dilbert in his cubicle hoping that no one will ever try to empower you to do anything, and five being that your attitude about getting things done is 'proceed until apprehended.' Then pass those cards to the front."

When Carol Jean's statistician completed her second calculation, she handed over a piece of paper with both averages. Carol Jean looked at the numbers and smiled. "It's the same everywhere I go," she said as she looked around the room. "You have rated your organization at 2.4 on the empowerment scale. But you have rated yourselves an average of 4.3." She feigned an expression of profound shock. "Ladies and gentlemen," she exclaimed with exaggerated emphasis, "that... is... not... possible! You *cannot* have a 2.4 organization filled with 4.3 managers. It's like Lake Wobegon, where all the children are above average. Not possible."

Carol Jean listened to the laughter and watched the exchange of murmured comments then said, "I administered the same survey to the executive team. What do you think the results were?" When no one ventured a guess she said, "The exact opposite. They gave themselves a 4.5 for trying to create an empowering environment, but rated people in the organization as being only a 2.7 when it comes to acting in an empowered manner. We have a bit of a disconnect here, don't we?"

Carol Jean asked everyone to pair up with a neighbor to discuss the exercise. Then she asked one person from each pairing to share their observations. She summarized what she'd heard by saying, "It sounds like we intend well but we execute less well." Hearing no disagreement, she proceeded. "If you knew it would change your life for the better, help you be a better manager, help you be a better parent if you're a parent, and create a much more positive and productive hospital environment, would you invest one minute a day in yourself every day for a year?" Some people nodded, some shrugged, and some sat with their arms crossed and did nothing, suspecting it was a trick question. "If you would," she continued, "if you're really serious about being willing to invest 365 minutes in yourself over the next year, please stand up." Carol Jean smiled inwardly. It was always the same. A few people – typically the ones who had nodded enthusiastically the first time she asked the question, popped right up. Then the ones who had only shrugged looked around to see how many were already on their feet and followed suit. Finally, feeling the weight of peer pressure, those who'd been slouched in their chairs with arms tightly-crossed slowly and with obvious reluctance pushed away from the tables and rose to their feet. "Well," Carol Jean said after verifying that everyone was indeed standing, "it's unanimous. So let's get started. Please take your seats and look in your I'm-Powered envelopes for *The Self-Empowerment Pledge.*"

> If you knew it would change your life for the better, help you be a better manager, help you be a better parent, and create a much more positive and productive hospital environment, would you take the *Self-Empowerment Pledge*?

When everyone had removed the small poster from their envelopes Carol Jean said, "*The Pledge* contains seven simple promises, one for each day of the week. Seven simple promises that will change your life. I didn't say that these promises can, might, could or should change your life – they *will* change your life, if you make them. And by standing just now, you've told me you're willing to make that investment in yourselves. So, can I please have a volunteer to get us started?"

To no one's surprise, Becki Smith – nurse manager for the newborn nursery – sprung to her feet before anyone else even had a chance to think about it. She was always the first to volunteer, even if she didn't know what she was volunteering for. "Thank you, Becki. Could you please read for our group Monday's Promise? And read it like you really mean it."

Becki squared her shoulders, took a long slow breath, then read. "Monday's Promise – Responsibility." She looked around the room before proceeding.

Most everyone was looking at her, several were reading the promises, and one or two were looking out the window with their arms crossed. With exaggerated self-assuredness, Becki read the promise:

I will take complete responsibility for my health, my happiness, my success, and my life, and I will not blame others for my problems or predicaments.

"Thank you," Carol Jean said as Becki sat back down to polite applause. "Now let me ask you all a question that I'll ask you to consider for each of these seven promises. Would MMC be a better place to work if every one of you made a good faith effort to live Monday's Promise?" Carol Jean folded her arms and looked around the room. There were nods, raised eyebrows, hopeful smiles, and a few expressions that didn't need words to convey "when pigs fly." She looked up at the clock, then back to the audience. "It takes about 15 seconds to repeat that promise. If you do it four times every Monday – morning, noon, afternoon, and evening – that's one minute. At first you might feel silly, making this promise to yourself. But if you keep making it, you will begin to see yourself as a person who *does* take complete responsibility for your circumstances and your outcomes. Think of it. No more learned helplessness, no more blame game. No more pretending to not be empowered. Would you all be willing to give up the time it takes to watch one TV commercial each Monday if you knew that would be the payback?" Carol Jean slowly scanned the room, silently willing each person present to make that commitment. "How about a volunteer for Tuesday's Promise?"

In the days to come, a consensus was reached that before this moment, no one had ever seen Nursing's IT manager Bill McMurphy raise his hand in a meeting. His hands were visibly shaking as he grasped the *Pledge* poster and his voice was little more than a whisper as he said "Tuesday's Promise – Accountability." Then, in a much more convincing manner, he read the promise:

I will not allow low self-esteem, self-limiting beliefs, or the negativity of others to prevent me from achieving my authentic goals and from becoming the person I am meant to be.

The applause this time was more enthusiastic, and Bill beamed as he sat down. "Thank you Bill," Carol Jean said. "Here's another question I want you all to think about for each of the seven promises: if you truly internalized and acted upon this promise, would you yourself be better off a year or so from now – personally, professionally, financially, and spiritually? If you're being honest with yourselves, the answer will be yes, absolutely." She scanned the room again. "Do I have a volunteer for Wednesday's Promise?"

Gertie Stein had been a member of the MMC family since starting as a candy-striper right out of high school nearly forty years earlier and until the day of her planned retirement the following year, there would be no question who was in charge of the operating rooms. "Wednesday's Promise is Determination," she said in a gravelly voice ravaged by a lifetime of smoking. She'd given up only when the medical center made the entire campus tobacco-free making it, she said, more trouble than it was worth to go find a place to smoke. Without pause, she launched into the promise:

I will do the things I'm afraid to do, but which I know should be done. Sometimes this will mean asking for help to do that which I cannot do by myself.

"You got that right," Gertie said as she sat down, then stood halfway back up to give a mock bow to the applauding group.

"Let me ask you," Carol Jean said, "is there ever any passive-aggressive behavior here at MMC?" The laughter and shouts of "Hah!" told her everything she needed to know: when it came to passive-aggressive behavior, MMC was very much like every other hospital she'd worked with. "Well, Wednesday's Promise is the antidote. Instead of feeling like martyrs because no one gives us what we've never asked for, we screw up our courage and we ask and we act. But we're more likely to get what we want if we couple Determination with Thursday's Promise on Contribution, so can I have a volunteer for that one?"

Several hands went up and Carol Jean pointed to a woman in the back row, closest to the door. She blinked hard, then kicked herself for not having been more observant. It was Sarah Rutledge, the nurse in the floral scrubs she'd met on that first morning in the cafeteria, the nurse who took care of little Timmy.

"Amanda couldn't be here today," Sarah said, looking acutely self-conscious as she rose to her feet, "she's at the AONE conference. So she asked me to sit in for her." Amanda Black was the nursing director for pediatrics. Sarah's boss.

Sarah and Carol Jean stared at one another just to the point of making everyone else in the room feel awkward before Carol Jean said, "Thanks for being here." Sarah looked down at the mini-poster, gave a quick nod, and announced that Thursday's Promise was for Contribution. Then she read:

I will earn the help I need in advance by helping other people now, and repay the help I receive by serving others later.

Sarah sat down to the heartiest round of applause yet. "That could be the nurse's credo, couldn't it?" Carol Jean asked. "If I had to state The Florence Prescription in just two words, those would be the two I would choose: helping and serving. But we nurses often forget that in order to help and serve, we need to occasionally ask for help ourselves, and to replenish our spirits. You cannot pour from an empty pitcher."

Carol Jean looked back at Sarah and visualized an invisible seat belt strapped across her waist, preventing her from bolting through the door before the meeting had ended. *You need her to fight with you, not against you. Win her over and the others will follow.* Carol Jean recalled what Nightingale had said about Sarah that first morning in the cafeteria. "Thank you, Sarah, for volunteering – and for being here." Sarah nodded half a nod and smiled half a smile, as if to say *that's all I'm going to yield to you for now*, but that was enough. Carol Jean made a mental note to ask about Timmy during the break, then said, "Friday's Promise is especially germane in today's healthcare climate; who wants to read that one?"

Again, a number of people raised their hands and Carol Jean pointed to Bonnie Wilson, who had recently been appointed director of education for the nursing division. "Friday's Promise – Resilience," she read, then laughed and looked around the room. "From everything I've been reading, things aren't going to get any easier any time soon, so I think this is one we all need to take to heart." She did a quick toe-stand, then read the Resilience Promise:

I will face rejection and failure with courage, awareness, and perseverance, making these experiences the platform for future acceptance and success.

"You know," Carol Jean said as Connie took her seat to more applause, "it's easy to feel empowered, it's easy to be motivated, when everything is going well. It's also substantially irrelevant. If things are already going great, who needs an extra jolt of inspiration? It's after you've run into the brick wall and fallen on your face that it's most difficult to re-empower, to re-motivate yourself to keep moving. But it's precisely at those times that self-empowerment and self-motivation can have the greatest impact. Unfortunately, if you wait until you need it to start working on it, it's probably going to be too late. Now, it's easier to keep Friday's Promise if you couple it with Saturday's. Do I have a …" Carol Jean didn't even finish the sentence before Jerry Rathman jumped out of his chair.

"Saturday's Promise is Perspective." Rathman was a Vietnam Veteran and recovering drug addict who now ran MMC's drug and alcohol treatment unit. The CEO previous to Myerson had tried to close the unit for financial reasons, provoking a fight that Rathman said was tougher than anything he'd ever faced in the Marine Corps. A fight he'd ultimately won. It was common knowledge that he was almost pathologically afraid of speaking in front of an audience. But today he spoke with the power of conviction, and experience.

Though I might not understand why adversity happens, by my conscious choice I will find strength, compassion and grace through my trials.

Rathman acknowledged, and was clearly a bit uncomfortable with, the applause as he returned to his seat. Carol Jean thanked him then said, "When I look back on the difficult experiences I've had myself, I can now see how each and every one of them was really that proverbial best thing that ever could have happened. One of my favorite book titles is *Thank God Ahead of Time* by Michael Crosby. I've tried to remember to do that every time something I don't like happens. How about a vol…"

"I'll do Sunday." Mitzi Farber was out of her seat, *Pledge* in hand, before Carol Jean finished the sentence, so she just nodded for her to go ahead. "Sunday's Promise is Faith."

My faith and my gratitude for all that I have been blessed with will shine through in my attitudes and in my actions.

"Amen," Mitzi said as she sat down, sparking a chorus of amens from people scattered around the room including, Carol Jean noticed, Sarah in the back of the room; she no longer seemed to be inching her way toward the exit. As director of the burn unit, Mitzi had daily opportunity to appreciate how most people take for granted such simple things as being able to pick up a spoon or walk up a flight of stairs, and to never have to go through the agonizing pain of debridement.

"Thank you, Mitzi, and all of our other volunteers," Carol Jean said. "Now, let me ask you all to think about this question: If everyone at MMC made a good faith effort to really live these seven promises, would you do a better job of serving your patients, your community, and each other?" Carol Jean noticed more emphatic nods, and fewer crossed arms, this time around. "And if we each worked at living these promises ourselves, wouldn't we do a better job of managing our time and money? Wouldn't we be better parents and happier human beings?" More nods this time, and Carol Jean noted that even the ones who'd been most obviously disengaged were at least no longer looking out the window with their arms straight-jacketed in across their chests. "And would you all be more effective managers? The answer to all of these questions is, of course, absolutely – how could it be otherwise?"

> If we each do our part, we will change our lives for the better. If we all do our parts, we will change our organizations for the better.

Carol Jean turned and looked up at the banner on the wall, then back to the audience. "So here's my last question. When I asked if you would invest 365 minutes in yourselves over the next year and you all stood up, did you really mean it? Will you really make these promises to yourself four times a day for a year? If you do, then 68 managers making a promise four times every day for 365 days means a total of 99,280 promises will be made. If you each do your part, you will change your lives for the better. If we all do our parts, we will change our organization for the better."

Carol Jean called a break, and after chatting with several of the nurse managers at the front of the room, wandered to the back corner where Sarah was sitting alone, nursing her cup of coffee. "Mind if I join you for a minute?"

"It's a free country," Sarah replied with a grin. "Sit anywhere you want."

Carol Jean turned a chair to face Sarah, then sat down. "How's Timmy doing?"

Sarah's face clouded over. "Not too good. Dr. Hayes isn't very optimistic. But you know, Timmy really is a brave little soldier. He still just might prove the docs wrong. It's happened before." Sarah sipped her coffee and contemplated the tips of her shoes. "You should have had Timmy here this morning. Let him give the speech. These seven promises… He lives them every day. More than most of us do. We could all learn a thing or two about life if we listened to Timmy Mallory."

The thought of Timmy losing his fight, and of the world losing Timmy, filled Carol Jean with a sudden overwhelming sadness. With it came a visceral appreciation of how Florence Nightingale must have felt every single day at Scutari, each of the thousands of times she lost one of her brave soldiers. "On Friday, we're having a retreat with the executive team." Carol Jean said. "You know – the suits," she added with a smile. "It's going to be at the Jupiter Lodge. If he's up for the trip, would you be willing to bring Timmy out? Just for a half-hour or so, to share some of his wisdom with the group. Maybe about 9:30 or so?"

Sarah nodded. "I could do that. Long as you don't expect me to say anything."

"No problem. I think once Timmy starts talking, we'll all just be listening."

When everyone had returned from their break, Carol Jean and Linda Martinez led a discussion on how individual managers might use *The Self-Empowerment Pledge* themselves, as professionals, as managers, and as people. As a concluding gift, Carol Jean gave everyone a framed copy of *The Pledge* and encouraged them to place it conspicuously on their walls or desktops.

THE SELF-EMPOWERMENT PLEDGE
Seven Simple Promises That Will Change Your Life

Monday's Promise: Responsibility

I will take complete responsibility for my health, my happiness, my success, and my life, and will not blame others for my problems or predicaments.

Tuesday's Promise: Accountability

I will not allow low self-esteem, self-limiting beliefs, or the negativity of others to prevent me from achieving my authentic goals and from becoming the person I am meant to be.

Wednesday's Promise: Determination

I will do the things I'm afraid to do, but which I know should be done. Sometimes this will mean asking for help to do that which I cannot do by myself.

Thursday's Promise: Contribution

I will earn the help I need in advance by helping other people now, and repay the help I receive by serving others later.

Friday's Promise: Resilience

I will face rejection and failure with courage, awareness, and perseverance, making these experiences the platform for future acceptance and success.

Saturday's Promise: Perspective

Though I might not understand why adversity happens, by my conscious choice I will find strength, compassion, and grace through my trials.

Sunday's Promise: Faith

My faith and my gratitude for all that I have been blessed with will shine through in my attitudes and in my actions.

❖ ❖ ❖

After the session ended, Carol Jean stayed for a while to discuss implementation strategies with Martinez and her lieutenants. Then she returned to the hospital to eat dinner in the cafeteria. But first she made a stop by the chapel. Florence Nightingale was already there, deep in thought. Carol Jean took a seat next to her and they sat in silence. Finally, without looking up Nightingale said, "The doctors are doing all that they can for our brave little soldier, but all they can do might not be enough. So between now and Friday, you need to work with him."

"I need to work with him? Doing what?"

Nightingale gave Carol Jean an exasperated look. "Why, teaching him to be a motivational speaker, of course. Wasn't it your idea to have him give a speech for the executives on Friday?"

"Yeah, well…"

Nightingale cut her off with a wave of the hand. "You all keep talking about patient-centered care, but sometimes you seem intractably unable to put yourselves in the shoes of your patients. If you can't see the world through their eyes, how can you possibly know what they really need? And if you don't know what they really need, how can you possibly place them in the center?"

Carol Jean resisted the temptation to be argumentative and simply asked, "What is it Timmy really needs?"

"To feel needed, of course. And to feel special. That's why it's so important that when he comes to your retreat on Friday, Timmy feels ready and confident. Right now, Sir Timothy Dragonslayer is perilously close to giving up on himself. He needs something more, something the doctors cannot give to him. In your speeches, you always talk about how important it is for people to have a vision and a sense of purpose. We caregivers often forget that our patients need that as well. Help Timmy find his vision and his purpose. Do that and he will once again become Sir Timothy the Dragonslayer."

Carol Jean was now alone in the chapel. She thought of her own father, after he'd had his stroke. It wasn't the stroke that killed him, she knew. It was the feeling of uselessness once his dreams of retiring to Arizona to play golf, and of volunteering for Rotary projects in Latin America, were no longer possible. She picked up a Bible and turning to the Book of Proverbs read, "Without vision, people perish." Then she turned to Ecclesiastes and read, "Whatever your hand finds to do, do with all your might." Carol Jean replaced the Bible and opened her portfolio. She had to make final preparations for the upcoming leadership retreat. Then she would go help Sir Timothy Dragonslayer get ready for his moment in the spotlight.

CHAPTER ELEVEN

It was a slow day on Pediatric Oncology, one of those rare days when Sarah felt she could take a real lunch break rather than eat on the run. She grabbed her lunch sack and the paperback she'd been reading and made her way back to the staff lounge, a former patient room at the end of the unit. Phyllis Brockman and Cindy Maron were already there. Sarah sat in the lounge chair by the window and opened her book. She had no intention of reading. This was her way of letting people know she wanted to be left alone. But she couldn't help overhearing what the other nurses were talking about in that confined space.

"Kevin Driscoll is having an affair," Phyllis told Cindy with the assuredness of one who has inside information. Cindy looked aghast, and shook her head in disbelief. "It's true!" Phyllis insisted. "I didn't want to believe it myself, but Martha saw him with his new little fling at Maxine's. She said it was plain as the nose on her face they have a thing going."

Cindy sighed sadly. "Who's the chick?" Phyllis looked over at Sarah to make sure she was reading her book, which she pretended to be doing, then leaned forward and with a conspiratorial whisper said, "It's that new nurse on 5 East, the one from New Jersey."

"No!" Cindy pressed a hand to her heart. "Does Ruthie know?"

"Not yet. But I wouldn't want to be in his shoes – or whatever those little sandal things he wears are – when she finds out."

Sarah closed her book and stood up to leave. Dr. Driscoll was with the largest internal medicine group in town. Some of the nurses called him Hollywood because he looked a lot like Brad Pitt. His wife Ruthie was a nurse in the surgical intensive care unit. Sarah knew he always took new nurses on his unit to lunch at Maxine's to get to know them, and to lay out his expectations. She'd have been willing to bet a month's pay, which she certainly could not afford to lose, that's what Martha had seen going on between Driscoll and the new nurse from New Jersey.

"It's so typical," she heard Phyllis say as she headed toward the door. "The wife puts the guy through medical school and residency, and then he trades her in for some sweet young thing as soon as he's making the big bucks."

Sarah dumped her lunch sack in the trashcan on her way out. Then she walked down the hall to Room 819 – Timmy Mallory's home away from home. The TV was on, but Timmy wasn't watching it. He was propped up against two pillows looking out the window. His lunch sat untouched on the over-bed table.

"What's the matter, Timmy? Not hungry?"

Timmy looked up at Sarah, down at the lunch tray, then back at Sarah. "Would you eat that?" he asked with a grimace.

"Probably not," Sarah replied. "It's Taco Day in the cafeteria. You want to go down with me?"

Timmy's countenance immediately brightened. "Yeah!" Just as quickly, though, his face fell. "I don't think the diet cops will let me out for a taco."

"No problem." Sarah walked over to the corner and opened up the wheelchair, then pushed it over to Timmy's bed. "We'll just tell them we're going down to sit by the fountain. What they don't know won't hurt them. And I know for a fact that eating a taco or two won't hurt you." There were no diet cops at the nurse's station as they wheeled their way past.

Carol Jean was sitting alone at a table by the window on the far end of the cafeteria. "Should we go sit with Ms. Hawtrey?" Sarah asked Timmy, noticing that every other table was occupied. With Timmy's enthusiastic endorsement, she wheeled him through the crowd toward Carol Jean's corner. They passed by a table where the new nurse from 5 East was engaged in animated conversation with several other nurses and one of the Internal Medicine residents. Sarah immediately felt guilty for having listened to the gossip upstairs, like some part of her soul had been spattered with mud.

"Can we join you?"

"Certainly!" Carol Jean stood and pushed one of the chairs out of the way for Timmy's wheelchair, then laughed and added, "It's a free country – you can sit anywhere you want to."

"How many tacos and what kind of milkshake?" Sarah asked Timmy as she positioned him at the table.

"Two and strawberry," he replied with his trademark smile. Then he turned to Carol Jean. "Hi Ms. Hawtrey. We haven't seen you upstairs for a while. Are you afraid the dragons will get you?"

Carol Jean laughed. "No, Timmy, as long as you're up there, I know I'll be safe from dragons. But I promise, I'll come back up tomorrow. You have a speech to get ready, young man, and I'm going to help you." Carol Jean and Timmy talked about dragons while Sarah made her way to the taco bar. "But I need a real sword," Timmy said. "The dragons aren't afraid of that yardstick any more." Carol Jean made a note on her pad. "Let me see what I can do."

Sarah returned bearing a tray with six tacos, a strawberry milkshake, a large cup of coffee, and a large vanilla latte. She placed two tacos and the milkshake in front of Timmy, and two tacos and the cup of coffee at her own place. The remaining two tacos and the vanilla latte she gave to Carol Jean. "I wasn't sure if you'd eaten yet. And vanilla is your latte of choice, right?"

"You read my mind! Thank you." In truth, Carol Jean had skipped breakfast and would probably have skipped lunch as well, and actually did feel as though Sarah had read her mind. Sarah was just about to start on her second taco when she saw one of the medical unit nurses walk into the cafeteria and head straight for the table where the new nurse from 5 East was sitting. She didn't sit down, just bent over and whispered something to the new nurse, who covered her mouth with both hands and shook her head in disbelief. The medical unit nurse nodded affirmatively and said something else. Then the new nurse from 5 East burst into tears and ran out of the cafeteria.

"I wonder what that was all about," Carol Jean said.

"Rumor's going around that she's having an affair with one of the doctors." Sarah said. "I guess she just found out about it."

Carol Jean was about to ask if the rumor was true, then thought better of it. After a moment of silence Timmy said, "I'm not the only one with cancer. This whole hospital has cancer."

"What do you mean, the whole hospital has cancer?" Carol Jean once again marveled at how perceptive Timmy was, and how often one of the side effects of childhood illness was adult wisdom residing in a child's body.

"Just listen to what they talk about. They're always complaining about something or talking about someone. I'm the one who's dying, but you wouldn't know it listening to the way people talk around here."

Carol Jean and Sarah looked helplessly at each other while Timmy glared at the seat just vacated by the new nurse on 5 East.

"You're not going to die, Timmy." Florence Nightingale had just occupied the fourth seat at their table. "But you are right about the emotional cancer in this hospital – in fact, in most hospitals."

Timmy seemed not in the least surprised by Nightingale's sudden appearance. "I mean, it really makes me feel bad, just listening to them. The doctors say I'm s'posed to be positive, but it's hard when some of the people around me are so negative."

"Iatrogenic toxic emotional negativity," Nightingale said.

"Iatro-what?" Timmy asked.

"Hospital-induced," Carol Jean answered the question. "Iatrogenic means something bad that was caused by the hospital, like if they give a patient the wrong medication and make him even sicker than he was."

"Or kill him," Nightingale added with a disgusted frown. "People of your time have so much, yet too often appreciate so little."

Sarah looked at Nightingale, who with her stern visage, Victorian black dress and white bonnet reminded her of an old schoolmarm posing in an ancient photograph. Then she looked around the cafeteria. Nobody else seemed to have taken note of Nightingale's presence at the table by the window.

"You cannot see toxic emotional negativity," Nightingale said, "but that doesn't mean it can't harm you. Quite the contrary."

"It's the spiritual equivalent of cigarette smoke," Carol Jean said. "At one time not so long ago, this cafeteria would have been polluted with a dense cloud of toxic tobacco smoke. Today we wouldn't tolerate even one person lighting a cigarette because we've come to appreciate how pleasant it is to breathe fresh air. Now, if we could eradicate toxic emotional negativity – all of the criticizing, complaining, finger-pointing and rumor-mongering – it wouldn't be long at all before we'd appreciate just how toxic that stuff really is. Then we'd never go back. And we'd never have to see a scene like the one we just saw."

> Toxic emotional negativity is the spiritual equivalent of cigarette smoke in the air – as harmful to the soul as smoke is to the body. Just as we once eradicated toxic smoke from our hospital environments, it is now our obligation to eradicate toxic emotional negativity.

"It's not true, by the way," Nightingale said.

"What's not true?" Carol Jean asked.

"The question you stopped yourself from asking. That poor nurse has just left a resignation letter on her supervisor's desk, and now she's sitting out in her car in the parking lot crying. She knows that even though it's a lie, people in this hospital will always look at her as the loose woman who had an affair with a married doctor. She'll become a very good nurse, that one will. Just not here."

Timmy shook his head and frowned. "It's not fair."

"Of course it's not fair," Carol Jean said. "That's why we need a conspiracy to eradicate toxic emotional negativity from this hospital." She looked at Sarah and nodded.

Sarah shook her head. "I still don't want to be part of any conspiracy."

Nightingale stood up. "Would you like to experience toxic emotional negativity in its harsh actuality? To see what can't be seen and hear what can't be heard, so as to know why so many people here often feel so bad?"

Sarah shook her head no, but Nightingale ignored her. She extended one arm in front of her and held up her hand, palm out. Sarah suddenly felt as if she'd stepped through a threshold into a different universe. She could simultaneously hear every conversation in the cafeteria. People were complaining about parking, about their doctors, about hospital food, about too much work and not enough money. They were talking about other people, making excuses and pointing fingers. "Stop it," Sarah said, but Nightingale just stretched her other arm. Now Sarah could hear every conversation going on throughout the hospital. "Stop it!"

The cacophonous chatter grew louder, like the approach of a marching band or a freight train thundering down a tunnel. Sarah looked down at Timmy, who had covered his ears and was shaking his head back and forth in obvious pain. "Stop it!" she screamed at the oblivious faces in the cafeteria. The noise built to a crescendo, beating against her the way sound waves might pound on a person trapped inside a giant bass drum. Timmy was squeezing his hands against his ears and screaming, tears running down his cheeks. "Stop it!" Sarah shrieked. She picked up her coffee cup and flung it out toward the oblivious faces. "Stop it! Can't you see what you're doing to him!"

The cafeteria was instantly silent as a mountaintop. Sarah felt an ineffable sense of peace, the peace of sitting alone on a sunlit beach. Then, as suddenly as reality had seemed to lurch off into another dimension, everything was back to normal. Sarah's coffee cup still sat steaming on the table in front of her, Timmy was drinking his milkshake and the cafeteria chatter was still going on, as if nothing had ever happened. "After experiencing the pain, and then the peace, you just felt," Nightingale said, "why would anyone even go back to that?" She nodded in the direction of the cafeteria crowd. "That's why we need this bottom-up conspiracy that Carol Jean talks about. Because if enough people like you scream 'Stop it!' to the complainers and the finger-pointers and the gossips, you can clear the air of toxic emotional negativity. You owe it to your patients. You owe it to each other. You owe it to Timmy. You owe it to yourselves and to your families."

Sarah took a slow deep breath, closed her eyes, and tipped her head slightly upwards with a serene smile on her face. When she opened them again, Nightingale was gone. Carol Jean and Timmy were both looking at her expectantly. "So," Sarah said resignedly, "I've never been part of a conspiracy before. How do we go about getting it started?"

CHAPTER TWELVE

The QILT Room was a spacious area on the seventh floor that had been reclaimed and remodeled when the Endoscopy Clinic moved into newer facilities downstairs. The walls weren't decorated with the patchwork quilts that were always a big hit at the annual black tie charity auction, but rather with large poster displays filled with charts and graphs. Titles in big black letters announced "Nursing Strategies to Prevent Nosocomial Infection in a Tertiary Level Burn Center" and "Cost Savings Derived from an Expedited Triage Process in an Urban Emergency Department." The members of the Quality Improvement Leadership Team – the QILT – had immersed themselves in the art and science of process improvement; most of them had their names on professional journal articles.

Today, Carol Jean was going to tell them that their work would soon reach a point of diminishing returns, and that unless they broadened their focus in some of the ways she would describe, they ran the risk of becoming functionally obsolete. Looking around the room as she waited for the meeting to start, she braced herself for a tough sell.

The meeting was chaired by Dale Prokopchuk, head of the Management Engineering department. He watched the second hand sweep around the clock on the wall, and at precisely nine o'clock called the meeting to order. "Before I introduce our guest, let us, as we always do, begin by reminding ourselves why we are here." Then, in unison and with no apparent sarcasm or irony, the group recited their mission statement: "We are committed to process quality improvement to achieve the best possible outcomes at the lowest possible cost in every area of MMC operations."

Carol Jean clapped when they had finished, genuinely impressed with their obvious enthusiasm. Prokopchuk went around the room and introduced each of the QILT's nine members, then explained that QILT members didn't do all the work themselves, but rather led interdisciplinary teams to work on specific projects. "Our goal," he said, "is to achieve the genius of an 'AND' solution – improved quality *and* reduced cost – and to never settle for the tyranny of an 'OR' solution in which we make a trade-off between the two. You are familiar, I assume, with the concept described by Collins and Porras in the book *Built to Last*?"

"Yes, I am," Carol Jean replied. "And that's actually a good starting point for my remarks. I've been reading about your work in the reports John Myerson sent me, and I'm impressed with your accomplishments. So in my comments I won't be suggesting that you make any 'OR' tradeoffs, but rather that you add a new 'AND' to your process matrix. But before I get to that..." Carol Jean stopped mid-sentence and looked around the room. "No coffee?" She'd come straight from a coffeeless meeting with a group of doctors and was already starting to feel withdrawal set in.

"We're a work group, not a coffee klatch," Prokopchuk said, but even as he was speaking Geraldine Gamble – who Carol Jean recognized as the food service director – gave her a wink as she made a call on her cell phone. "It's on the way." Smiling at Prokopchuk she said, "Caffeine is the drug of choice for people of genius."

"I'm sorry, I really didn't mean to..." Carol Jean stammered, "it's just that you sort of get to expect a coffee pot when you come into a morning meet..."

Geraldine cut her off with a laugh. "Honey, when we took a vote, it was eight for and one against." She looked over the top of her glasses at Prokopchuk. "And your vote just tipped the scales in our favor."

"Alright, alright," Prokopchuk said, holding both hands in the air and shaking his head, "you win. Coffee it is. But I'm drawing the line at donuts." Then in another break with regimented tradition, he allowed small talk to continue until the coffee arrived. Several minutes later someone from food service entered the room pushing a cart with a pot of coffee and a dozen ceramic cups (MMC had recently discontinued Styrofoam for environmental reasons), and was clearly surprised to receive a standing ovation.

Once everyone had their coffee and had settled back into their seats, Carol Jean continued. "It's a classic truism that our greatest strengths can go full circle and turn into weaknesses. But understanding weaknesses can help you be more creative in developing strengths. IBM's dominant strength in mainframe computers became a serious weakness when the personal computer arrived on the scene. Their inability to compete in the PC market, which had become a commodity business driven by downward cost pressures, sparked renewed emphasis on a strategy of delivering high-end business solutions, not just hardware. It saved the company."

Carol Jean sipped her coffee and wished that she had, in fact, asked for donuts before Prokopchuk had drawn his line in the sand. "One of the first signs that a strength might be turning into a weakness is when you see it reaching a point of diminishing returns. Across the country, we're seeing quantitative methods reach that point. In the best-run organizations, low-hanging fruit has been picked and, to mix my metaphors, future quantum leaps in service quality and productivity will have to come from somewhere else."

A stranger walking into the room at that moment might have surmised from the looks on people's faces that Carol Jean had announced that Elvis was alive and well, and that she'd had breakfast with him just that morning.

Terry Armistead, MMC's director of Pharmacy Services, was first to rise to the challenge. "I'm sorry, Carol Jean, but I just can't go along with that. There will always be opportunities to improve quality and efficiency. Contrary to popular impressions," he added, looking around the room with a smile, "the spirit of Dr. Deming is alive and well here at Memorial Medical Center.

Carol Jean nodded. "Please don't misunderstand me. I am not saying that statistical process improvement doesn't have a place. It does and always will. What I *am* saying is that, unless you expand the definitions of your mission, you will inevitably reach that point of diminishing returns and run the risk of becoming increasingly irrelevant. In fact, that's already happening. Even now, this group is struggling to find the 'home run' sorts of projects that seemed to be everywhere when you first started. Am I not correct about this?"

In one of her graduate school courses, Carol Jean remembered the professor as having said "silence is acquiescence." Assuming acquiescence from the group's silence, she continued. "Terry, you mentioned Dr. Deming. Something else he said is that the most important number in any organization cannot be counted. I'm going to challenge you to expand your mission to include those things that really count, but which cannot be counted. In other words, to expand your focus from the left brain emphasis that has traditionally defined process improvement to a more bicameral approach that incorporates both sides of the brain, left and right."

> Left brain and right brain are metaphors that represent important aspects of the organization's culture. Left brain and right brain are endpoints on a continuum; it's not left brain OR right brain, it's where you fall on that continuum, and whether it makes sense to move in one direction or the other.

"I think I know the distinction between left brain and right brain, Carol Jean, but can you give us your definition?" It was Bill Templeton, a masters-prepared nurse who headed up the medical center's case management function.

"Sure. In fact, let's spend some time on it, because the left brain-right brain dichotomy is central to a lot of what we'll be doing together. As I always say, the left brain counts and the right brain matters. They are both important, counting and mattering, but American business, including the business of healthcare, is way too heavily tilted toward the left brain." Carol Jean opened her portfolio. "I've got a simple handout that will help us look more carefully at how the distinction applies to organizations." She started the one-page handout going around the room. It had two columns. The header at the top of the left-hand column said "Left Brain" and the header at the top of the right-hand column said "Right Brain." Underneath each column was a series of blank lines. Once everyone had a handout she continued. "As we go through this, please keep two things in mind. First, since we're talking about an organization rather than an individual, we're using left brain and right brain as metaphors to represent important aspects of the organization's culture. Second, left brain and right brain are endpoints on a continuum; it's not left brain OR right brain, it's where you fall on that continuum, and whether it makes sense to move in one direction or the other."

Carol Jean finished her coffee as she gave the group a chance to look at the handout. "As I go through this, please write a one or two word descriptor on each row under the two headings, plus any other notes you want to take. Let's start with the first row. Under the left brain heading please write the word 'linear,' and under the right brain heading write the word 'relational.' In terms of patient care, left brain sees the patient as a heart attack or a broken leg, which is the root cause of our ultra-specialized and highly-fragmented healthcare system. Right brain, on the other hand, recognizes the interconnectedness between the heart and the leg, and sees the patient as more than a broken body needing to be fixed; it knows there is most likely a hurting soul inside that broken body. In terms of hospital leadership, left brain is lines on the organization chart; right brain is the complex matrix of relationships through which informal leadership and influence are exerted. Again, it is not linear OR relational, it is linear AND relational; the question is where you fall on the continuum."

She was pleased to see that everyone had written down the words "linear" and "relational" on the first lines under each heading, and that most people were making additional notes as well. "On the second line," she continued, "left brain is rules, right brain is values. When people share values in common, you don't need a lot of rules to dictate behavior. You might be familiar with the well-known policy manual at the Nordstrom department store chain, which simply says that employees are to use their best judgment in every situation, and that there will be no further rules. This works at Nordstrom because everybody buys into a common set of core values. On the other hand, when people do not share values, you need a lot of rules."

This particular point was, Carol Jean knew, where efforts to foster an empowering organization were most likely to get bogged down. Managers who were steeped in the traditional command-and-control model often resisted efforts to replace rules with values. "Here's another way of looking at it," she said. "When people's attitudes and behaviors are shaped by a set of commonly-shared values, you can treat them like adults. You don't require an adult to give you a doctor's note to stay home with a sick child because if they buy into your values, they won't abuse the privilege by acting like a child playing hooky. But you can see where this can be one of the biggest stumbling blocks in moving from a culture of accountability toward a culture of ownership. A great deal of bilateral trust is required." Carol Jean noticed about an equal number of approving nods and doubtful frowns. She paused for a moment to allow the note-takers to catch up, then continued.

"On the next set of lines, under left brain write 'process' and under right brain write 'attitude.' You can *hardwire* process, but you must *softwire* attitudes. Most of your projects have been remarkably successful, but there was one that, at least according to the report John shared with me, was a total bomb. Does anyone know what I'm talking about?"

Most everyone nodded and John Watkins, director of the maintenance department raised his hand. "When we changed the policy to allow people to perform minor maintenance chores, like changing light bulbs, without having to call down to my department."

"What happened?" Carol Jean asked.

"Well, it made total sense to let people do for themselves here at the medical center the things they do for themselves at home. But lots of people upstairs felt like they were being put upon, being given chores not in their job description, and some of my guys felt like their job security was being threatened. The whole thing just sort of fell on its face."

"So a very intelligent left brain process improvement idea was undermined by the absence of right brain attitudinal buy-in?"

"That's about the size of it."

"And that gets me to the next row. Left brain is *accountability*, right brain is *ownership*. Have any of you ever checked the oil in a rental car?" Everyone chuckled and shook their heads no. "Of course not. You are accountable for bringing the car back with a full tank of gas, so you do, but there's no pride of ownership so you don't check the oil or take it through the car wash. Any time you hear someone say something like 'not my department,' any time someone walks by a piece of paper on the floor without stooping to pick it up or past a patient call light without at least sticking their head in the room to see what the patient needs, that person is just renting a spot on the organization chart, they aren't taking ownership for the work. When I mentioned this to John, he said you have a lot of people renting jobs here at MMC." This time there were assenting murmurs all around the room.

"And this gets us to the distinction between management, which is left brain, and leadership, which is right brain. Please write those two words on the next row. I'm sure you've heard that management is doing things right while leadership is doing the right things. By that definition, QILT's current role is management. However, here's another way of looking at the distinction: management is a job description, leadership is a life decision. Indeed, some of the most influential leaders in any organization don't actually have a management job title. They are leaders because they see what needs to be done, they're willing to take the initiative, and they're able to influence others to work with them. By that definition, I believe there is significantly greater potential for the QILT to play a leadership role at MMC than what you have assumed thus far."

> Some of the most influential leaders in an organization don't have a management title. They are leaders because they see what needs to be done, they're willing to take the initiative, and they're able to influence others to work with them.

Carol Jean tried to take a sip from her empty coffee cup, then set it back down on the table. Immediately, Geraldine Gamble popped up to refill it. Carol Jean smiled in appreciation. "That, ladies and gentlemen, is what you call servant leadership," she said, earning a collective chuckle. "And getting back to the distinction between management and leadership, when you get right down to it a manager is a boss, while a real leader is a servant. It's a beautiful paradox, isn't it? The best leaders aren't bosses, they're servants."

Carol Jean sipped her coffee as Geraldine went around the table refilling everyone else. "The next line is where, for this group at least, the rubber hits the road. Creating plans is primarily a left brain activity, so write the word 'planning' in the left-hand column. But inspiring people to take ownership for those plans, and to do their part to successfully implement the plans, is an activity of the right brain, so write 'inspiration' in the right-hand column. Looking back at the maintenance example, this group did all of the left brain stuff exactly right. I read the plan you put together and could find no fault with it. The problem was that people out there on the floors were never inspired to own the plan, to do their part to make it work. Almost every organization I work with has 3-ring binders filled with strategic plans that have never been fully implemented because no one really understood that there's a significant element of cheerleading in leadership. Before a plan can – as Peter Drucker famously said – degenerate into work, people need to be inspired to take ownership for that work." At this point, Dale Prokopchuk looked at his watch and said, "It's 10:15, why don't we inspire ourselves with a 20-minute break so we can take care of emails and all that other left-brain stuff." Smiling at Carol Jean he added, "I'm just taking ownership for my role as chief cheerleader of the QILT."

Proud of herself for having learned her way around, Carol Jean hiked up the back stairway and came out at the end of the Pediatric Oncology unit on the eighth floor. The door to room 819 was partway open, so she walked in. Timmy's bed was empty; Florence Nightingale was seated in the rocking chair in the corner, eyes closed and hands folded, appearing to be either deep in thought or sound asleep. Carol Jean was about to tiptoe out when Nightingale said, "They took him to intensive care. He is not reacting well to this latest round of chemotherapy. He will be alright, so long as they let him keep killing dragons. Did you talk about that in your meeting? How important it is to let little boys kill dragons?"

"Not yet, but I'll make a point of it. Is there anything I can do for Timmy?"

"Yes," Nightingale replied. "He needs a better sword." Carol Jean wasn't sure if that was intended as a joke, but didn't have the chance to ask since the rocking chair was now empty. She went back down the stairs to the seventh floor, but her heart went out to the pediatric intensive care unit with a prayer for little Timmy Mallory.

When Carol Jean came back into the QILT conference room, there was a blueberry muffin and a fresh cup of coffee at her place on the table. Geraldine gave her a wink and a thumbs up and whispered, "Thanks for your vote." Carol Jean ate her muffin and finished the coffee as she waited for the rest of the group to arrive.

When everyone had settled in, Carol Jean resumed going through her handout. "On the next row let's consider a paradox of the left brain, right brain dichotomy: you can measure left brain qualities, but you can't see them. If a 'bottom line' walked into this room right now, what would it look like? That's a preposterous question, of course; the things we measure are for the most part statistical abstractions. On the other hand, we've all had the experience of walking into a department store and being confronted by a clerk who says all the right words, like she's memorized a script, but says them with a sourpuss attitude. That negative attitude cannot be measured, but you sure can see it, can't you? And when it comes to patient satisfaction, the things we measure are less influential in how patients evaluate their stays than are the things which can be seen but not measured. So our challenge, and the challenge to the Quality Improvement Leadership Team, is to come up with new ways to assess those things which can be seen but cannot be measured. Such

> The things we measure are less influential in how patients evaluate their stays than the things which can be seen but not measured. Invisible right brain factors largely determine patient and staff satisfaction.

things as the emotional climate of this organization, what it feels like to be cared for here, what it feels like to work here."

Carol Jean had met Richard Fenton, the director of planning, on her first day and knew he would be hard to win over. When she'd learned that he was a member of the QILT, she reminded herself to take the advice that she so often gave to others and be a Dionarap, a word that as far as she knew she had made up. It was the word "paranoid" spelled backwards, a reminder to always assume the best of everyone in every situation. So when Fenton raised his pen, she nodded in his direction with a smile. "What you're saying makes sense in theory," he said, "but how do you suggest we assess whether or not people smile enough, or measure whatever emotions they might bring to work with them?"

"That's a great question, Richard. I'll have more suggestions at the leadership retreat on Friday – you are planning to be there, right?" Fenton nodded. "Great. For now, I'll just say that while you might not be able to empirically measure something like friendliness on a five-point scale, you can use observational methods to get a pretty good feel for it. But as I said, I'll go into greater depth on Friday. Okay?" Fenton nodded, but Carol Jean could tell he had yet to be convinced. And she was sure he wasn't the only one.

"The next row has huge implications for leadership. Under the left brain heading, please write 'a given' and under the right brain heading please write 'a choice.' Here's what I mean by that. When I woke up this morning, I could not decide that 'today I think I'll be a neurosurgeon, or maybe an accountant.' Those professions require a substantial investment in left brain training. But when I got out of bed, I *did* make the choice of whether I was going to have a good day or a bad day, and so did all of you. And we continue to make that choice, many times each day. Here's why that's so important for you in your leadership roles." Carol Jean paused and looked around the room. Everyone had pen in hand and curious looks on their faces. "If you want to transform your organization by focusing on left brain qualities, it takes a substantial investment of time and money. People don't *decide* to have a graduate degree, they *earn* a graduate degree. But if you focus on right brain qualities, you can have an immediate transformative impact, just by raising your expectations and lowering your tolerance level for deviations from those expectations."

Fenton set down his pen and shook his head. "Give me an example. I'm not sure I'm with you."

"Okay," Carol Jean replied, "here's one from outside of healthcare. Michael Abrashoff was a young Navy officer whose first command was one of the worst rust buckets in the service. It had scored near the bottom on every quality index, and its retention rate was zero; every single sailor jumped ship as soon as his term expired. One of the first things Abrashoff did upon taking command was to give his men an order that any time someone came aboard their ship – and he emphasized that it was *their* ship – they were to smile, extend their hand in greeting, and say 'Welcome to the best damn ship in the Navy!' Within a year, the ship was setting records for quality, and retention had soared from zero to one hundred percent. And it all started with raising right brain expectations. That's an example of organizational transformation that begins with a focus on things that can be seen but not measured. Does that help?"

"What was his name again?"

"Michael Abrashoff. He wrote a book called *It's Your Ship*, which is where I learned about his story."

Fenton wrote the title down on his handout. A good sign, Carol Jean thought to herself. "Here's a related point. Left brain is inert, right brain is contagious. Please write those words on the next row. I'm spending my morning in a room with a group of people who have incredible quantitative skills, but I know I'm not going to 'catch' one iota of that ability from you. On the other hand, we've all had the experience of having one negative, bitter, cynical, sarcastic pickle-sucker walk into the room and suck the energy right out of everyone who's already there."

"Pickle-sucker?" Dale Prokopchuk asked the question, but he wasn't the only one with a quizzical expression.

"Oh, sorry, that's the name I give to people who look like they were born with a dill pickle stuck in their mouths." Carol Jean puckered her face into a cartoonish caricature of toxic emotional negativity and everyone laughed. "You've heard the saying that one bad apple spoils a barrel. It's the same thing with people. One toxically negative person can drag down the morale and the productivity of an entire work unit. One of the most frequent questions I'm asked when speaking is some variation of this: 'How can I prevent the negative people I work with from dragging me down with their toxic emotional negativity?' Whenever I hear that question, my first thought is there's a failure of leadership in that person's organization. If someone comes to work in the morning wanting to work hard and do a good job, and wanting to go home at the end of the day physically tired but emotionally uplifted, we're not doing our jobs as leaders if we allow the pickle-suckers to take that away from them."

> One toxically negative person can drag down the morale and the productivity of an entire work unit. It is a core leadership responsibility to create a workplace environment where toxic emotional negativity is not tolerated.

Angela Tierney shook her head in disagreement. She was nursing director for critical care. She had published many articles on both clinical and management subjects, and was a no-nonsense, results-oriented leader. "I don't buy it. Each individual is responsible for her or his own attitude. To blame the pickle-suckers, as you call them, for the fact that you're having a bad day is a copout. It's also a contradiction to the notions of self-empowerment that you shared with us in the nursing leadership retreat."

Carol Jean leaned back in her chair and thought for a moment before she responded. "I agree with you that we must be responsible for our attitudes, Angela, but we're also more susceptible to being influenced by those around us than we often care to admit. Over time, we cannot help but be influenced by what sociologists call our reference group – the people we spend time with, the people we relate to. Speaking for myself, anyway, if I have to spend a day in a room full of negative people – pickle-suckers – it drags me down. Here's another way of looking at it: I am personally responsible for my health. But if someone comes into this room and lights a cigarette, they are causing me harm. Today we have rules that prevent people from doing that, but at one time my only options would have been to breathe the poisoned air or to leave the room – which might have meant having to quit my job. That's a pretty good metaphor for toxic emotional negativity, which is the spiritual equivalent of cigarette smoke. When we allow it to permeate the workplace, we're telling people that they either have to put up with it or leave. Does that make sense?"

Tierney thought for a second then nodded. "Okay, I'll buy that."

Carol Jean looked at her watch. They had only fifteen minutes left (she'd been told that QILT meetings always started precisely on-time and ended precisely early). "The next-to-last line is a bit different in that it does refer to a specific process. John Myerson sent me a copy of your group's study of the challenges you'll face with recruiting and retention in the very near future. Congratulations, it was very well done." Carol Jean took a few seconds to look at each person around the room individually. The QILT study did, in fact, accurately describe the problem that quite soon there would be too many healthcare jobs chasing too few healthcare professionals, and offered some very workable suggestions. "There was only one problem with your report," she added.

"And what was that?" Dale Prokopchuk asked the question after Carol Jean had let her comment hang in the air several seconds too long for his liking.

"You did not address the fact that recruiting and retention require you to hit very different motivational hot buttons. I call it the Honey and Glue formula; you recruit with the 'honey' of measurable inducements like pay and benefits, job title and opportunities for advancement, and so forth. But you earn loyalty with the 'glue' of such qualities as a spirit of fellowship on the work unit, pride in the organization, and engagement in the work itself. So please write 'Recruit with Honey' under the left brain column, and 'Retain with Glue' under the right brain column."

Molly Anderson was director of human resources, and while she'd hardly said a word all morning, she had been taking copious notes. Now she smacked her forehead with a dramatic flourish. "Ach! I'm so used to saying recruiting-and-retention as a single word that I'm afraid we might not be doing either justice by recognizing that they actually work on opposite sides of the brain." She glanced over at Prokopchuk. "This really makes a lot of sense." Then looking back at Carol Jean she added, "I should have figured this out myself."

"Don't feel bad about it. It had never dawned on me until one of my clients pointed it out. And this is related to the last line on the handout. Left brain is what you do; right brain is who you are. Whether you are recruiting caregivers or marketing to potential patients, people will come to you because of your reputation as a medical center. But over time you will earn, or not earn, their loyalty by who you are. When I move to a new community and need to find a doctor, I'll go to the Yellow Pages or Google, or talk to my neighbors. I'll make my first appointment because she is a family doctor. But over time, I'll stay with that doctor, and refer her to others, only if I know, like, trust and respect her. In other words, not because of what she does but because of who she is. Today more than ever, clinical excellence is assumed. People take it as a given that you are good – very good – at what you do. So the defining source of competitive differentiation is more likely to be cultural than it is to be technical."

There were only a few minutes left, and Carol Jean could already see Dale Prokopchuk starting to file his notes into the big black portfolio he almost never let out of his sight. "Before we go," she said, "please draw one more set of lines at the bottom of the handout. I'll conclude by saying that all left-brain is boring, while all right-brain is chaos. An important part of the art of leadership is knowing how to balance, and how to integrate, the two."

Looking around the room Carol Jean sensed, or at least she hoped, that QILT members had been convinced they should add more of a right brain component to their work. She concluded by saying, "I believe that most hospitals, MMC included, are overbalanced on left-hand side of the brain. The good news is there's tremendous opportunity to cultivate those right brain qualities, and that in being the first to do so you can create a sustainable source of competitive advantage. Even better news: it will be fun." Carol Jean looked at the clock on the wall. She had finished with twenty-two seconds to spare. "I look forward to seeing you all at the leadership retreat on Friday."

The left brain counts and the right brain matters

LEFT BRAIN	RIGHT BRAIN
Linear	Relational
Rules	Values
Accountability	Ownership
Management	Leadership
Creates plans	Inspires people
Measurable	Seeable
A given	A choice
Inert	Contagious
Recruit with honey	Retain with glue
What you do	Who you are
Boring	Chaos

As people were leaving, Geraldine motioned Carol Jean over to the corner. As soon as the last person had left the room she said, "Dale likes to put on that he has two left brains, but he's really very creative. He also has a heart the size of a football field. Don't you worry about Dale, he's going to come around just fine."

After packing up her things, Carol Jane walked to the intensive care unit to visit Timmy, but he was sleeping and the nurses did not want him disturbed. Then she went down to the executive offices. "Hi, Connie, is John around?" She picked out four green M&Ms from the jar on Connie's desk.

"No, he's in a meeting."

"Imagine that, a hospital administrator in a meeting."

"Yeah, tell me about it. I schedule them all. Hey, do you mind if I ask you a personal question?"

"Sure, go ahead. But I reserve the right to not answer."

"Why do you just pick out a certain color of M&Ms? Can you really tell the difference?"

Carol Jean shook her head. "No, they taste all the same to me. But that's the problem. If I were on death row and they asked me what I wanted for the menu of my last meal, it would be six pounds of M&Ms. This is just a little game I play to keep myself from inhaling the entire dish." As she was answering the question, Carol Jean had been writing a note for Myerson. "Would you give this to John when he gets back?"

Since Carol Jean hadn't folded the note over, Connie read it. "A sword? Why do you want him to buy a sword?"

"Oh, I think he'll know. How are you doing on your supply of M&Ms? Do you need me to pick some up for you when I go to the grocery store this afternoon?"

Connie laughed. "Wouldn't sending you out for M&Ms be sort of like sending a recovering alcoholic to the bar to buy me a bottle of gin? But don't worry about it, Carol Jean, I've got a stash of M&Ms that would have fed half the Roman Empire."

CHAPTER THIRTEEN

Thursday morning Carol Jean slept in. Her first meeting was not until 10 o'clock, and by the time she'd gotten to bed Wednesday night it was, once again, well after midnight. Over a leisurely cup of hotel room coffee, she responded to e-mails, made a few telephone calls, read the headlines of several online newspapers (just to make sure the world hadn't come to an end while she slept), and then for 45 glorious minutes she turned out the lights, set her iPod to play Brahms' fourth symphony, and stretched out on the recliner with another cup of coffee.

Her thoughts drifted back to her first day on the job as a staff nurse on the internal medicine unit of a large teaching hospital, more than thirty years earlier. Before she'd even learned how to log in on the employee time clock, much less where everything was located in the crash cart, one of her patients (whose name she had only just learned but would never forget) had coded. The chief resident was jack-hammering compressions into the patient's chest, and screaming at Carol Jean to get something – she had no idea what – out of the crash cart, but she couldn't even figure out how to unlock the drawers. After what seemed like hours, but was probably no more than five seconds, the charge nurse raced into the room, shoved Carol Jean out of the way and took over managing the code. An hour later, they wheeled the body to the morgue.

Walking through the nurse's station that afternoon the chief resident said to the charge nurse, loudly enough that everyone else behind the counter could hear, "Internal Medicine is no place for candy-stripers. What's the matter, can't you find any real nurses?"

Studying the patient's chart before she went home that evening, Carol Jean realized that nothing short of Jesus walking into the room and pulling another Lazarus miracle could have saved that desperately sick old man, but she still could not shake the feeling that his death had somehow been her fault. The next day, Carol Jean told the charge nurse that she really didn't think she was cut out to be a nurse and intended to resign. "Lesson number one, Carole" the charge nurse replied, looking up from her desk, "is never take anything personally. That's just the way Dr. Thompson is; it's the way a lot of them are. It's how these docs cover up for their own fears of being inadequate to the task. Get used to it, Carole. You'll do fine."

"It's Carol Jean."

"What?" The charge nurse had redirected her attention to the piles of paper on her desk, obviously expecting that Carol Jean would already be on her way out the door.

"My name is Carol Jean. Not Carole." The charge nurse rolled her eyes and went back to her inbox. "Whatever," she muttered as she signed another form.

Carol Jean felt a hand gently shaking her shoulder. "I know your name is Carol Jean." It was Florence Nightingale, and the Brahms symphony was over. Carol Jean struggled to sit up straight, then remembered that she had to pull up on the lever of the recliner in order to put the leg rest back down.

"What time is it?"

"It's almost nine o'clock."

Carol Jean stretched and rubbed her eyes. "The meeting's at ten, right?"

"This one is especially important," Nightingale said. "Remember, there is never a revolution without resistance, and for some of the people in that room, this will be a revolution indeed." Nightingale smiled grimly. "Though had your contemporaries ever witnessed barricades being erected by angry mobs in the streets of Paris, they might be more careful in how they use that word revolution."

Carol Jean took a quick shower and got dressed. When she came out, Nightingale was seated at the kitchenette table with a steaming cup of tea. Carol Jean noticed a Post-it note stuck on the top of her portfolio:

"What's this?"

"It's a reminder," Nightingale replied.

"A reminder for what?"

"A reminder that you have two ears and one mouth, and that for a consultant as for a caregiver it's twice as important to listen as it is to talk. The ability to listen, observe and understand is much more important than the ability to prescribe. In fact, asking the right questions and then probing to understand the answers is usually the first step toward the correct prescription."

Carol Jean reached the hospital with just five minutes to spare. "Hi Connie," she said as she charged into the executive office suite. "Are the others here yet?"

"Yep. They're waiting for you down in the back conference room."

Carol Jean picked four green M&Ms from Connie's dish, then started down

> Asking the right questions and then probing to understand the answers is usually the first step toward the correct prescription.

the hall. "Good luck," she heard Connie say and wondered whether she would need it. She walked slowly down the corridor toward the back conference room, munching M&Ms and mentally rehearsing the speech she was planning to give. Myerson had told her that the decision to engage Hawtrey & Associates for this project was a management prerogative, not subject to union input. However, he'd added, he wanted her to make the union's leaders feel like partners in the process. He told her that unions represented MMC's nurses and maintenance workers. Without union support they would not achieve their full potential, and with active union resistance they could be dead in the water. Carol Jean shuddered at the metaphorical image of being dead in the water as she stood outside the conference room door finishing her last M&M. This was the first time she'd worked in a unionized environment, and without even realizing it she'd been conjuring up mental images of Jimmy Hoffa and a crew of knuckle-popping Teamsters waiting for her behind the door.

She took a slow deep breath, opened the door, and stepped inside. There were seven people clustered around the coffee counter, already engaged in lively conversation. Carol Jean recognized most of them from her wanderings around the hospital. There were four nurses, three in uniform and one in street clothes, two guys from the maintenance department, and a woman in a business suit Carol Jean did not recognize. "Hello, I'm Janet Musgrove from the State Nurses Association," said the woman in the suit, extending her hand. "I've been looking forward to meeting you ever since I read your book. In fact, I brought my copy along. If you don't mind, I'd love to have you autograph it."

"Be happy to," Carol Jean responded, and silently reminded herself to refrain from making assumptions about other people on the basis of superficialities, like what side of the bargaining table they happened to sit on during negotiations.

"What motivated you to write *Leadership Lessons*?" Musgrove asked as Carol Jean was inscribing the title page.

"Good question! Of course, being a nurse I was fascinated by the woman most of us look up to as having been first in the profession. The more I learned, though, the more I appreciated that it was really in her role as manager and as leader that Nightingale achieved her most lasting influence. In many respects, she was also the first professional hospital administrator. And since no one else had written a book focused on the leadership aspect of the Nightingale legacy, I decided I would."

"I'm glad you did. I wish more healthcare professionals would read it. A lot of things would be different if we all took those lessons to heart."

"A lot of things would be different if Miss Nightingale was in charge, that's for sure. But there's something else about Florence that has me more impressed than her nursing and leadership abilities – something I've come to appreciate since writing the book."

"What's that?"

"She truly believed that since we are all children of the same God, we deserve to be treated with dignity and respect. She would not allow different levels of care for Anglicans and Catholics, or for officers and enlisted men, even though that sort of discrimination was common in Victorian England. I think that's why she moved with equal grace through the palaces of London and the soldiers' tent city on the battlefield of Balaclava. She wasn't awed by titles and she wasn't put off by their lack. I'm confident that, were she to come back today, Nightingale would be impressed by our sophisticated technology, but not by the way we pigeonhole each other on the basis of the superficialities she worked so hard to look past."

"Maybe you should write a book about that."

Carol Jean pursed her lips in contemplation. "After I typed 'The End' on the manuscript for *Leadership Lessons*, I swore I'd never write another book. But maybe I'll break that promise. You think Florence would mind?"

"How could she? She's been dead for a hundred years."

Carol Jean stepped a bit closer toward Musgrove. "This is going to sound silly, Janet, but when I was working on the book, I lived in fear that if I got it wrong, Florence would come back and haunt me. Pretty ridiculous, huh?"

"You must have gotten it right, since that didn't happen."

Carol Jean laughed. "I don't know about that. She shows up on my dreams with some regularity. But at least the publisher's happy." She handed Musgrove back her newly-autographed book. "Shall we get started?"

Carol Jean made a quick circuit around the room shaking hands then, with a last stop at the coffee pot, took her seat at the head of the table. "Well, thanks again for coming this morning. Did you all get Mr. Myerson's letter explaining why I'm here?" Everyone nodded. "Good. We want to make sure you're informed about what we're doing. More important we're hoping to draw on your wisdom and ideas, and hopefully your support of our efforts to cultivate a more positive organizational culture. So I guess my first question would be, how are union-management relations from your perspective?"

"We've never had a strike, if that's what you mean." It was Bill Bristow, the shop steward in the maintenance department.

Carol Jean nodded and steepled her fingers. "That's good! Is there any question in your minds as to whether there might be one in the future?"

Janet Musgrove shook her head emphatically. "We certainly hope not. Nobody wins in a strike. Especially not the patients." Musgrove looked around the table without smiling. "But without having the threat of a strike in our back pocket, before long you can have management trampling on the rights of labor. Like's happening in some of the other hospitals we haven't organized yet. So while we all hope it won't ever happen here, we'll never say never. Depends on how management treats us."

"Well, these new guys seem to be okay. They're sure a lot better than the last crowd we had in here." Jane Rodgers had been at MMC for 32 years, most recently (which she said meant for the past 27 years) as a nurse in Labor & Delivery.

"*New* guys? Myerson's been here three years." Carol Jean drummed the fingers of her left hand on the table and rested her chin in the palm of her right hand, then realized that this was the body language of a bored and imperious manager, which was the last thing she wanted to convey in this meeting, so instead she leaned on her forearms and laced her fingers together to keep them still.

"They're still on probation," said Bristow.

"Still on probation? How long does someone have to be here before they're off probation?"

"We'll let you know," said John DuPont, the other maintenance guy. Everyone laughed, including Carol Jean.

"So how are the new guys better than the last crowd?"

Bobbie Jackson was a nurse in the operating rooms. She was the one Carol Jean had never seen before, but she was quickly struck by her quiet intensity. "I think they listen better. And they don't automatically side with the docs no matter how outrageous their behavior is, the way the old administrator did. I guess they do a pretty good job of letting us know what's going on, except we never see any of them down in OR. Except for Linda Martinez. She's the best thing that's ever happened to this hospital." The other nurses nodded their agreement.

"You're lucky to have her. But why do you say she's the best thing that's ever happened here?"

"She doesn't put up with B.S." Shari Levenger was the nurse in street clothes. She worked in the outpatient clinics. "In this place it's always been a few people doing most of the work, while everyone else gets paid the same for just coasting by. They talk about accountability being one of our core values, but Martinez is the first person to take it seriously. This place could be so much better if everyone would just do their job and cut out all the pettiness."

At that moment, you could have blown Carol Jean over with the sneeze of a hummingbird. The last thing she'd expected coming into a meeting with union people was someone chiding management for not holding people accountable for doing their work. "Can you give me an example?"

Levenger thought for a moment. "Yeah. We do free cancer screenings twice a month. Some of the clinic nurses didn't want us to get into that, and when they got assigned it was like trying to make a rock smile. Patients sometimes waited for more than an hour while they gabbed in the break room. So we ended up changing the schedule around so those nurses didn't have to do it anymore. Which meant the rest of us had to pick up the slack. When Martinez found out about it she had a fit. When the next schedule came out, the load was spread fairly. And the day of the next clinic, Martinez came down and talked to every patient in the waiting room. Believe me, we got the message."

"That's great," said Carol Jean, "but I have to tell you, I'm surprised to hear this. I hope you all won't take this wrong, but I thought part of the role of a union was to – how do I say this? – to make sure people aren't being overworked."

"You mean featherbedding," Musgrove said.

"Uhm, yeah, well at least that's what they called it in the labor management textbook we used in the nursing college."

"We don't want a free ride," Levenger said, "we want a fair ride."

Rob Chance was a trauma nurse who also flew with the Memorial Flight emergency helicopter. "Do you want to know why so many of us say it's 'Why Care?' instead of I-CARE?" Carol Jean nodded. "Because we're not sure *they* care. They tell us we can't afford a daycare program for the staff, then they put that new fountain out in the courtyard. Maybe they've got a good reason, but all we ever hear down in the trenches is the same public relations shtick that goes into the brochures."

"It's not just stuff like daycare," said Bill Bristow. "Try getting a requisition approved for a new power drill. The bean-counters send it back with a 50-page questionnaire you gotta fill out to justify it. Last time I really needed something, I finally just went down to Lowes and bought it myself. But when we had to put in the new projector system for the boardroom? Man, that was top of the line, and they wanted it installed STAT."

Carol Jean was making notes. "What I'm hearing you say is you don't feel like the administration is really listening to you when it comes to the things you really need, and they're not communicating very effectively about why they're doing what they do. Is that fair?"

Bristow nodded. "That and a pay raise."

Carol Jean smiled and shook her head. "I'm only talking about culture. You'll have to take the pay raise issue to the bargaining table." She set down her pen and looked around the table, making eye contact with each person. "What has to happen in this place so that nobody ever says 'Why Care?' again? So that everyone truly buys into I-CARE?"

There was a long silence as they each looked around at the others in the room, waiting for someone to speak up. At last, it was Bobbie Jackson from the OR. "You already know the answer to that, Carol Jean. If they want a culture of ownership, they need to treat us like we're owners. Treat us like we really are partners in the enterprise, not just hired hands doing the work. It's that simple."

"Can you give me an example? Tell me about a situation in which you don't feel like you're being treated as partners, and how it could be handled differently."

"Sure. Something that's going on right now. You know there's been lots of layoffs in this area. That means some of us are, at least for a while, sole breadwinners for our families. So naturally, we wonder how secure our jobs are. If you listen to the rumors - and trust me, there's lots of rumors flying around – there could be layoffs at MMC. Now I'm not too worried for myself because I know how hard it is for them to find good OR nurses, but the

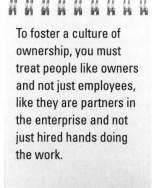

To foster a culture of ownership, you must treat people like owners and not just employees, like they are partners in the enterprise and not just hired hands doing the work.

people I work with are my friends. And when they feel like they've been left hanging, not knowing if they're going to have a job next month or not, it brings everyone down."

"The danger," interjected Janet Musgrove, "is that you can create a self-propelling downward spiral. People start worrying about if they're going to keep their jobs, and that drags down productivity and hurts patient satisfaction, and so administration tightens the belt even more. Which causes even more anxiety and on and on."

Bobbie Jackson nodded her agreement. "We understand, we really do, that they can't guarantee our jobs. But that's not what we're asking for. We just want to be treated like adults who can be trusted to handle the truth. I don't want to hear 'don't worry' and I don't want to hear 'we don't know.' I want them to tell me how many surgeries we did compared to a year ago, and how we're doing compared to the other hospitals in town. I want to know what's keeping them awake at night so I can stop losing sleep I don't need to lose. I want to know the same things they want to know – what's the bottom line?"

"I'm on the school board," said Rob Chance. "We meet every month and they give us detailed financial statements. Now, being on the school board is important work, but it's not nearly as important to me as being able to put my kids through school, which is what my hospital paycheck does. That and not much else," he added with a big grin. "Since so much of my life is wrapped up in this hospital, and quite frankly since I give so much of my life to this hospital, you would think they'd give me at least as much information about how we're doing as I get for my volunteer, once-a-month commitment to the school board. But they don't."

"Have you seen the *Memorial Memo*?" asked Bill Bristow. Carol Jean nodded tentatively. They'd sent her several back issues of the employee newsletter with the mountain of paper she'd received several days after signing the contract and she'd thumbed through them, but there had been nothing particularly memorable. "It's a joke," Bristow said. "It's a waste of paper and the money they spend sending a photographer around trying to catch people smiling so they can take their pictures." Bristow slumped into his chair and clasped his hands behind his head, legs stretched out in front of him. "It's not a newsletter because there's no news in it. They aren't telling us nothing except who's won the latest happy face prizes."

"I'll give Myerson and Martinez credit, though," Janet Musgrove said. "I think at least they're trying. It's more than the managers at some of the hospitals we're in are doing. It says something that you're even here meeting with us, Carol Jean. But if they're serious about this culture of ownership thing, they need to be doing a lot more. And I'm not just talking about the employee newsletter."

Looking up at the clock, Carol Jean decided not to pursue Musgrove's comment. Instead, she laid down her pen and said, "Thank you. This is very helpful. We're going to need to wrap up in a minute, but one last question. Is there a particular message you want me to make sure I deliver in my final report?"

"Yeah," said Bristow. "Tell them we're all in this together."

On her way back down the corridor, Carol Jean stuck her head in Myerson's door. He was on the phone, but waved for her to come in and close the door behind her. She pulled up the chair in front of his desk. He was, she could tell, on the phone with Dr. Warren. *This could take awhile*, she thought to herself. She contented herself with scanning over the items on the casework behind his desk. There was the usual assortment of management textbooks every CEO had to show off to visitors, plus a number of titles Carol Jean hadn't seen before. She made note of several titles for her next visit to Amazon. com. The green-and-white football reminded her that Myerson was a fanatical Michigan State sports fan, so she made another note to remember this at Christmastime. There were two family pictures: Myerson and his wife Sandy on a sailboat in apparently tropical waters, and Myerson with his two sons at the Grand Canyon, with all three carrying elephantine backpacks.

"Alright, I'll look into it," Myerson finally said before hanging up the phone. He leaned back in his chair and rubbed his temples with his fists in obvious exasperation. "Doctors!" He spit out the word as if "doctors" was appropriately positioned between "cockroaches" and "scorpions" in the dictionary. "So," he said after rubbing his forehead, as though to rid himself of the memory of Dr. Dracula, "did you survive your time in the lion's den?"

Carol Jean leaned forward with her elbows on Myerson's desk and rested her chin on her fists. "John, you have a problem."

Myerson took on an immediate expression of concern. "Why? What happened in there? What did they say to you?"

Carol Jean looked up at the green-and-white football for a long moment, then back to Myerson. "I didn't say that *they* have a problem, John. *You* have a problem."

"What do you mean, I have a problem?"

"When I asked your union reps what message they would like me to transmit to administration, they said to remind you that we're all in this together. But what was it you asked me after you got off the phone with…" she nodded toward the telephone, "with, what do you call him, Dr. Dracula?"

Myerson frowned. "I just asked you about your visit to…" He leaned back in his chair and clutched a fist to his chest. "To the lion's den. Arrgghhh!"

Carol Jean nodded. "It's not just you, John. I've been trying to figure it out, this feeling I get from your team, and I think it's that, in a very subtle way, you're all in a sort of battle-mode mindset, seeing the world as us-versus-them. And unfortunately, probably without your even being aware of it, certain pain-in-the-neck doctors and pain-in-the-neck union reps might slip over into the 'them' category."

Myerson slumped back into his chair and shook his head. "I guess this is what I get for hiring an insultant in consultant's clothing. But you know, I'm afraid you might be right."

"Diagnosis is the first step toward cure. Tomorrow we'll be working with your management team on the eight essential characteristics of a culture of ownership. Whether or not we are successful in making that transformation – moving from a culture of accountability toward a culture of ownership – will partly depend on whether your managers can look at difficult employees, or difficult doctors, and see fellow owners and not just pains-in-the-neck."

Myerson looked down at the calendar on his desk and scratched his head. "Sandy and I are having the Executive Council over for dinner tonight. It was supposed to be just a casual social get-together. No business agenda. But I think we'll have a little chat about changing the way we respond to people like Dr. Dracula. Beginning with me. And that's the last time you'll ever hear me refer to Dr. Warren like that again."

"And the last time you'll refer to the lion's den?"

"It's a promise."

"Good. One more thing. You know what they said when I asked what they most wanted from administration?"

"More money?" Carol Jean put her hands on her hips and glared. "Just kidding! Tell me what they said."

"More time. Specifically, more of *your* time. They want to see you up on the floors, down in the shop. Not just passing through every now and then, but on a regular basis, telling them what's going on, answering their questions. In a word, treating them like owners, not like employees."

"Money is tight, Carol Jean, but time is tighter." He gazed over at the blueprints hanging on his office wall and it was clear that he was weighing his next words very carefully. At last he said, "I know you're right. Let's make sure that one of the things that comes out of our leadership retreat tomorrow is a commitment that we leaders will spend more time with people and less time in meetings."

"Excellent. Like I recently heard someone say, we're all in this together."

On her way out, Carol Jean stopped at Connie's desk and picked out four orange M&Ms. "Always four?"

Carol Jean smiled and picked out a fifth orange M&M. "It's been a good day. Let's splurge."

Connie laughed then said, "Wendy called to say that she'd meet you in the cafeteria at 6:30, but she has to be back on the job by 7:15. I sent her a copy of your book last week, and she said that she's already read it. Twice. I wish all of our board members were as enthusiastic, and as committed, as she is."

❖ ❖ ❖

Meeting with one or more members of the hospital board was part of Carol Jean's standard operating procedure, but they usually met for dinner at a fancy restaurant, not in the hospital cafeteria. As soon as the meeting was scheduled, she knew that board chair Wendy Harper was someone special. Harper had suggested the cafeteria because it was her evening to volunteer in the newborn nursery and she didn't want to leave "her" babies for too long. In her day job, as she put it, Harper was president of the Bohannon Agency, the region's largest public relations firm. She was also a cancer survivor who had raised millions of dollars for MMC's cancer center.

"Connie told me to tell you not to eat more than four at one time," Harper said, smiling as she pushed a bag of pink M&Ms across the table. "We're all looking forward to having you share your ideas at our board meeting when you come back next month. You know, John has a great sense of humor, and he tells me there's a possibility that Florence Nightingale might actually come with you. I hope she does, I would love to meet her."

Carol Jean wondered just what Myerson had told his board chairperson. "Well, from what I've learned in my studies, I'd say that Miss Nightingale had a mind of her own, and pretty much showed up when and where she wanted to. So who knows? Maybe she will make an appearance."

"That would be fun. But just in case she doesn't, we will all have read your book. I loved it, and am actually sharing it with my leadership team at the firm. And we'll probably end up getting copies for everyone. Those lessons apply to everyone, not just people in healthcare."

"I thank you and my publisher thanks you," Carol Jean replied.

"The eight essential characteristics of a culture of ownership are right on target. And they apply to every organization, not just hospitals. But you left one out."

Carol Jean unconsciously arched her eyebrows. "I did? What did I leave out?"

"You left out community. When you have a culture of ownership, people bring down walls, they reach out, they try to expand the community. In fact, that will happen almost automatically in an organization that has internalized the eight characteristics you describe in your book. Don't you think?"

Carol Jean picked up the bag of pink M&Ms and weighed it in her hand, then set it back down again. She drummed her fingers on the table and stared at the copy of *Leadership Lessons from Florence Nightingale* that Harper had laid on the table. Then she nodded. "Yes, you're probably right. This book," and she tapped the book with the tips of her fingers, " has done well. The publisher has asked me to start working on a sequel. My working title is something along the lines of bringing down the walls in healthcare. Which I suppose is another way of saying creating community. What do you think?"

"I like it. And the world needs it. I think you should write it."

Carol Jean walked with Harper up to the newborn nursery so she could be introduced to the evening shift staff, and to the babies. After making the rounds, she walked over to the pediatric intensive care unit. "Can I see Timmy Mallory," she asked the unit clerk, a young man who judging from the gigantic book he was poring over was a pre-med student trying to get a little real world experience.

"He's not here," he replied. "This afternoon he rallied big time. They sent him back to the onc unit. I hear that when he got back to the unit, he called down to room service and ordered some tacos and a milkshake."

CHAPTER FOURTEEN

The executive leadership retreat was scheduled for all day Friday at the Riverview Room of the Jupiter Lodge Country Club – though the club itself was more than 35 miles from the nearest river. The plan was for a full day session followed by a nice dinner, with Saturday open for golf, hiking, fishing or just sitting on the porch with a good book. The 32 invited guests included MMC's senior leadership team, three elected leaders of the medical staff, plus two representatives from the parent system's corporate office and Wendy Harper representing the MMC board of directors.

The room was set up with 16 small rectangular tables in two rows with an aisle down the middle. The tables faced forward but were angled inward so people could see each other without breaking their necks. There were two seats at each table. At the back of the room was a long table loaded with coffee and snacks (Jupiter Lodge was famous for its coffee cake). At the front was an elevated platform with a ramp leading up to the stage. On the wall hung a large banner with the words:

WE CARE

To the surprise of many and the relief of several, the room was not filled with flip-chart tripods and marker pens. At five minutes before nine, John Myerson asked everyone to refill their coffee cups and, if there was any left, grab another piece of coffee cake and take their seats. At nine o'clock he stepped onto the stage. "We've got a lot to cover today so let's get started. I believe that most of you have met Carol Jean Hawtrey, who will be facilitating our retreat, so she's the woman who needs no introduction. But we do have a special guest I want you to meet before we start." Myerson looked through the back door of the conference room where Sarah Rutledge was waiting out in the corridor with Timmy Mallory. He motioned for them to come in. As she pushed Timmy's wheelchair toward the stage Myerson said, "You might not be aware that Memorial Medical Center is infested with dragons. Fortunately for us, Sir Timothy Dragonslayer has been conducting a one-man dragon extermination campaign up on the eighth floor." Timmy blushed as Sarah wheeled him around to face the audience.

Myerson stooped to one knee. "Hi Timmy, are they taking good care of you upstairs?" Timmy nodded nervously and looked at the faces around the room. "We all appreciate what you're doing for us, Timmy, killing those dragons." Timmy nodded again, and looked as though he was having a hard time catching his breath. Myerson stood and walked over to the podium, then returned holding a long tray covered with a red cloth. He asked Sarah to remove the cloth, then presented Timmy with an exact replica of a medieval broadsword that was sized for the hands of a ten-year-old. Timmy lit up like a Christmas tree and took hold of the sword. "Timmy," Myerson continued, "we have a very important inspection coming up soon."

"You mean Jay-Ko?"

Myerson arched his eyebrows in surprise and looked out at his management team. "I think we have a future hospital administrator here. He already knows about Joint Commission."

"He's too smart to be an administrator," shouted Dr. Franklin from the back of the room. "Timmy, tell Mr. Myerson that you want to be a doctor."

Timmy smiled sheepishly as he looked up at Myerson. "I want to be a doctor."

"Well, when you get out of medical school, Timmy, there'll be a spot waiting for you on our medical staff. But you'll have to get Dr. Franklin to approve your credentials."

"No problem," Franklin bellowed and everyone laughed.

"So, Timmy," Myerson said, "we have this Jay-Ko inspection coming up, and it would look really bad if they found any dragons sneaking around the hospital. With this new sword, do you think you can take care of that for us?"

Timmy nodded. "I'll try."

"Whoa, young man, what's that I heard?" It was Sarah, standing beside his wheelchair. "Try? Did you say try? What does Yoda say about that word?"

"Do or do not. There is no try." Timmy tried to look fierce as he pointed the sword toward the back of the room.

"That's right. So what's your answer to Mr. Myerson?"

Timmy held the sword up in front of his face with both hands, tip pointed toward the ceiling, like a warrior about to be knighted by his king. "Yes, I will slay the dragons!"

When the applause finally died down, Myerson asked Timmy if he would say a few words before he went back to the Dragon Wars. "Okay," he said, not sounding in the least bit confident. Timmy looked around the room as he turned the sword over in his hands. "You guys all need a sword like this," he finally said. Then he sat still and silent in his wheelchair.

After a moment Myerson said, "Tell us why we all need swords, Timmy."

Timmy scrunched his face in thought the way 10-year-olds do then said, "Cuz you've got dragons too."

Myerson stooped to one knee. "What do you mean, we have dragons too, Timmy?"

"Like Jay-Ko, and… you know." He looked up at Sarah and shrugged, as if not knowing how to really get across what he was trying to say.

Sarah cleared her throat and tried to look serious, but inwardly she was laughing hysterically. For how many years had she wanted to give "the suits" a piece of her mind? And now her chance had come – they were all here in this one room, waiting to hear what she had to say. And what she was about to say was going to be very different from what she would have said just the week before. "I think what Timmy is trying to say is that we need to have a different perspective on the challenges we face. We need to see opportunities where others see barriers. We need to be cheerleaders when others are moaning doom-and-gloom. We need to have what Carol Jean calls contrarian toughness – being thankful for problems because it's in how we solve our problems that we differentiate ourselves from everyone else. That's why we need swords. Metaphorically speaking. The sword Timmy's talking about isn't a tangible blade, it's a positive attitude. It's contrarian toughness." Sarah looked down at Timmy and put a hand on his shoulder. "Did I get that right, Timmy?"

> We need to see opportunities where others see barriers. We need to be cheerleaders when others are moaning doom-and-gloom. We need to face problems with contrarian toughness because it's in how we solve those problems that we differentiate ourselves from everyone else.

Timmy nodded and looked out at the audience. "Since you guys are the bosses…" He looked up to Sarah and whispered, "They are the bosses, aren't they?" She reassured him that, yes indeed, he was talking to the bosses. "Since you guys are the bosses, you need to – you know, be like Aragorn. You need to fight your dragons, not just complain about them." Timmy looked quizzically at the audience then said, "Didn't you guys see *The Lord of the Rings*?" Now there were appreciative nods around the room, even from those who hadn't seen the movie or read the books. "That's what Miss Nightingale says. You've got to be brave and go fight the dragons."

Myerson scanned the room, then looked back at Timmy. "When all these guys go back to their offices on Monday morning, you want to know what they're going to find on their desks, Timmy? A sword just like the one you have. To remind them that we have to fight our dragons and never run away from them." Timmy nodded approvingly. Then he looked up at Sarah. "How'd I do?"

"You were brilliant, Timmy," she replied with an affectionate whisper. "You ready to go back now?" He nodded, and said goodbye to the leadership team by punching a hole in the air with his new sword. Carol Jean bent over and kissed Timmy on the cheek as Sarah wheeled him by, causing him to blush again. "Are you going to join us today?" she asked Sarah.

Sarah nodded. "Yeah, Amanda's still out of town so I'm filling in for her. One of the security guys is going to drive Timmy back to the hospital. I'll be in the back row – and you'd better not call on me, Ms. Big Shot Consultant." Sarah scowled and Carol Jean laughed, causing Sarah to scowl even more fiercely before she, too, broke into a laugh.

"Well," Carol Jean said, addressing the group as she waved goodbye to Timmy, "thank you all for joining us today. And for having me join you. We've got a big day planned. Over the past week, you've been asking me to tell you what The Florence Prescription is, and I've been putting you off, saying that there wasn't a simple answer to the question. Dr. Franklin has been teasing me that consultant's answers almost always start with 'yes *and* no,' and in that spirit the answer to the question 'what is The Florence Prescription?' is at once simple and complex. The simple answer is right up there," and Carol Jean pointed up at the WE CARE banner hanging on the wall behind her. "It's caring. Really caring – about our patients, about each other, about the organization. The more complex answer is the one we're going to work on today. The Florence Prescription is making the transition from a culture of accountability to a culture of ownership." From her seat in the back of the room, Sarah gave a surreptitious thumbs-up.

"In my book *Leadership Lessons*," Carol Jean continued, "I mentioned that Florence Nightingale corresponded with many of her literary contemporaries. Henry Wadsworth Longfellow wrote the poem *Santa Filomena* which immortalized Florence as the Lady with the Lamp. She and Charles Dickens shared the insight that whether it's the best of times or the worst of times depends upon the perspective you choose to give to the times. Another literary contemporary was

Mark Twain. Twain's most memorable character was, of course, Tom Sawyer. Does anyone remember how Tom got all the other kids to whitewash the fence for him?"

Several hands went up and Carol Jean pointed to Connie, Myerson's executive assistant. "He made it sound like so much fun they all wanted to get in on it."

"Right. Tom himself was being held accountable for getting that fence whitewashed. But he was not in a position to hold the other kids accountable for helping him. He had to create a sense of…" Carol Jean looked back at Connie and prompted her to finish the sentence.

"Ownership!"

"Bingo! That is the essence of effective leadership, and it is the heart of The Florence Prescription. Florence is best remembered for her work during the Crimean War, but some of her most enduring accomplishments – the reform of the British military health system, the use of quantitative epidemiological methods for hospital quality assessment, the Nightingale school of nursing, the first hospital that was specifically designed to be a hospital – all came about because she influenced other people to take ownership for the endeavors. She knew that the real role of a leader is to inspire other leaders. Followers are accountable, leaders take ownership. And, as I often say, in today's complex, turbulent and hypercompetitive world we need leaders in every corner, not just in the corner office. We need to move from accountability to ownership."

Carol Jean stepped over to the whiteboard at the back of the stage and picked up a black marker from the tray. "The genesis of *Leadership Lessons From Florence Nightingale* was a study I conducted when I was teaching at the nursing college. I wanted to know what it takes to create a more positive and productive culture within hospital nursing departments. The more I studied successful nursing organizations, the more clear it became that promoting a sense of ownership is crucial, and that this transcends nursing and applies to the entire organization. In every organization that successfully made the transition from a culture of accountability to a culture of ownership, we found these eight essential characteristics." Carol Jean wrote on the whiteboard:

Commitment

Engagement

Passion

Initiative

Stewardship

Belonging

Fellowship

Pride

"Today we're going to begin a process I call Cultural Blueprinting. In a minute, I'll have you break up into eight groups, one for each characteristic, and talk about what that characteristic means for us here at MMC. I'll ask you to come up with specific actions that we as a leadership team can take to show people that WE CARE," and she pointed up to the banner, "is more than just a slogan. Then in the afternoon I'm going to break you up into groups again with the challenge of drafting a succinct phrase that captures the essence of what you want your culture to be. A statement of cultural aspirations is just as important as a statement of values or vision, though virtually no hospital or any other organization ever goes through the process of thinking this through and then putting it down on paper or, taking it a step further, in a frame in the lobby."

> The core cultural characteristics that you define inevitably become central to the brand image of the hospital as it is perceived by the community.

Carol Jean replaced the black marker and returned to the front of the stage. "Some of you have heard me say that culture is to the organization what personality and character are to the individual. Just as you would want to guide your children in the development of character strength, doesn't it make sense that we should have a plan – a blueprint – for cultivating our desired culture for MMC? Notice that 'cultivate' and 'culture' share the same root word, cult, and recall that Jim Collins says organizations which are 'built to last' have 'cult-like' corporate cultures. A hospital is really a patchwork quilt of cultures – the culture in Nursing can be very different from the culture in Pharmacy, Food Service or the Business Office. And within Nursing you can have very different cultures on the medical floors, the ED and the OR, or on the day shift and the night shift. Given that, what are the non-negotiable core elements you want to be sure shine through in your culture, in every department? These cultural characteristics will inevitably become central to the brand of MMC, as it is perceived by your community."

Carol Jean put down the marker and surveyed the room. "Are there any questions before I send you off into your groups?" There were none. As the eight groups went off to their respective breakout rooms, Carol Jean refilled her coffee cup and cut off half a piece of coffee cake, then walked out onto the back deck. It was a gorgeous day with a soft southerly breeze. Florence Nightingale was standing at the railing looking off into the woods. "So, Miss Nightingale, just what did you say to Sarah Rutledge?"

"Why do you think I said anything to her at all?"

"I don't have any other way to explain the miraculous turnaround in her attitude over the past several days."

"She asked me a question, and I simply answered it," Nightingale said with a sly smile.

"And what might that question have been?"

"Sarah asked me what I would've done differently, if I could do it all over again – which, of course, none of us can ever do."

Carol Jean nibbled at her coffee cake and sipped on her coffee. "And what was your answer? What would you have done differently?"

Nightingale leaned forward against the railing and watched a hawk kiting lazily over the woods. "I told her that I would have been slower to judge other people, and quicker to forgive their slights, both real and imagined." Nightingale turned to face Carol Jean. "I told her that someday she would regret standing outside of the house throwing rocks rather than coming inside to help those working to make things better, even though they and their methods might be flawed. That's all."

"Well, thank you. It obviously worked."

"I wasn't just talking to her."

"Who else were you..." Carol Jean stopped mid-sentence when she realized that Nightingale was no longer there, and she was once again talking to the air. She also knew that she herself was the other person Nightingale had been addressing. After the divorce, her ex-husband had tried to build a new type of bridge between the two of them, but had finally given up when she never returned his phone calls or answered his letters. That same hard edge had also pushed away several potential business partners, assuring that Hawtrey and Associates remained a one-woman firm.

"Florence talked to you about her regrets, didn't she?" Carol Jean had not seen Sarah come out onto the porch, and was embarrassed to be seen crying. Sarah put an arm around her, and pulled a tissue from the pocket of her yellow sweater. "A good nurse is never without these," she said with a voice usually reserved for the little people she cared for on pediatric oncology. "Florence is right, you know. It really is nicer to be on the inside trying to help than it is to stand outside throwing rocks."

Carol Jean and Sarah were standing together at the porch railing looking off into the woods when Connie came out to tell them the groups were ready. "We'll be right there," Carol Jean said without turning around. She then turned to Sarah. "How do I look? Is it too obvious?"

With her two forefingers, Sarah gently pushed up the sides of Carol Jean's mouth. "There. Now you look just fine. Should we go see what they came up with?"

CHAPTER FIFTEEN

Carol Jean poured herself a glass of water and stepped back up onto the stage. Members of the management team were still engaged in animated conversations, and no one seemed in a hurry to resume the formal program. Sitting down on the edge of the stage, she sipped her water and contemplated what had just happened out on the porch. She somehow knew that Florence considered her work with Carol Jean and MMC to be nearly finished. She also felt the truth in Nightingale's message that in order for her to be effective at helping hospitals make the transformation she was prescribing, she would need to transform herself.

Out on the porch, the two fears that haunted Carol Jean had come to the surface. The first she thought of as the "right now" fear – the fear she would come back into a room like this following a break to find a note from the CEO telling her they'd all decided that she was wasting their time and had gone back to work. The fact that it had never happened, and obviously was not going to happen today, did little to assuage her anxiety that someday it *might* happen.

And then, standing on the porch with Sarah's arm around her shoulder, Carol Jean had realized that the long hours she put into making sure that her "right now" fear never did happen were insidiously contributing to her second, much bigger fear – her "someday" fear. Carol Jean was terrified that "someday" she might end up just like Florence Nightingale: a lonely old woman secluded in a tiny space of her own making, bounded by the walls she had created to keep people out of her life so she could concentrate her entire being on finishing her work. That "Hawtrey & Associates" would die with her, leaving behind only a few dusty books on library shelves. She smiled at the irony of it. The harder she worked trying to prevent the "right now" fear from transpiring, the more she contributed to the likelihood that her "someday" fear could become a self-fulfilling prophecy.

From the back of the room, Sarah was waving and pointing to her watch. Carol Jean was to have reconvened the group ten minutes ago. She nodded appreciatively then stretched her legs before climbing back onto the speaker's platform. *You need her to work with you, not against you.* The thought came to her in the voice of Florence Nightingale.

"I know you all are enjoying the conversations, and I hope they will continue long after our program today. But let's get back together now and share the ideas you've come up with. As I said, these eight characteristics are all essential to a culture of ownership, and there is no priority order to them. They each interact with and build upon the others. So who's going to be my first brave volunteer?"

Linda Martinez waved, then stood up. "I should go first since our group covered commitment, which we *do* see as the underpinning to everything else. In our view, a culture of ownership requires commitment to at least three things. Commitment to our shared values, to a common vision of the future we want to build, and to each of us doing our best to make this medical center the best it can be."

"Excellent," said Carol Jean. "Did your group have any specific suggestions for gaining this commitment?"

"Quite a few, actually. First, we think we should have an organization-wide training initiative on values. This should include the I-CARE values of Memorial Medical Center, but we also believe we should help people get clear about their own personal values, and what more they can do to act on those values. That's not only in their interest, it's also in the medical center's interest. People will act out our *organizational* values only to the extent they perceive them to be congruent with their *personal* values." Martinez looked around the room for questions or comments, then continued. "This training should be action-oriented, not just theoretical puffery. We should help people use their values to be better parents, to manage their time and money more effectively, to be happier campers all the way around."

Martinez leaned over and had a whispered exchange with Don Campbell, the director of medical imaging, who'd also been in the group focusing on commitment. Then she spoke to the group. "We had quite a spirited discussion on this next one, but in the end we all agreed that we should incorporate the I-CARE values into every job description and performance appraisal, and that we should expect every one of our caregiving partners – a term we like better than employee – to know them by heart. Beginning, of course, with the people in this room. But more than that, to understand what those values mean in terms of our expectations for their attitudes and behaviors at work. Anyone who is unwilling to embrace our values should be invited to work somewhere that has values they *can* embrace." Martinez nodded emphatically. "Tough-loving leadership."

> People will act out an organization's values only to the extent that they perceive them to be congruent with their personal values.

"Wow," said Carol Jean, leading a round of applause. "That was fabulous, Linda and group. I'm going to ask someone from each group to write up your notes and pass them to me." At this, Martinez ostentatiously handed her notes to Don Campbell, which he immediately passed like a hot potato to security director Bill Hartmann, who in turn barely touched them before shoving them into the hands of volunteer director Ginny Latroia, who finally took ownership, provoking hysterical laughter. Once things had settled down Carol Jean said, "Okay, who's next?"

Dale Prokopchuk rose from his seat with yellow pad in hand. "Our group worked on fostering a greater spirit of fellowship here at MMC. We really like the notion of creating a support group environment, one where at the end of the day people would go home physically tired but emotionally uplifted." He laid down his pad, stuck his hands in his pockets, and looked up at Carol Jean. "Most of the people here know this, but last year I lost my wife to cancer. While we were going through it, I don't know what we would have done without the friends we made in our cancer support group. It's like you said, Carol Jean, we never left the meeting without renewed hope and new friends. During the QILT meeting, you asked why our workplace can't be like this, and it's a provocative question."

Prokopchuk again picked up his yellow pad and reviewed his notes. "We think the best way to create that support group environment is by actually sponsoring employee support groups. But there are two preconditions. First, they need to be more than coffee klatches; there should also be a strong educational component. They should integrate right brain camaraderie with left brain learning. Second, they should be concerned with the things people really care about. In today's economic climate, that probably means that we should help people with their personal finances. We also talked about parenting support groups, since at least at our table we're sensing real concerns about kids' education today – or lack of education. We think participation in any hospital-sponsored support groups should be strictly voluntary, but...," Prokopchuk shot a glance at CFO Terry Barnes and continued, "if people do choose to participate it should be on hospital time."

Barnes smiled and lifted his palms in a "who me?" sort of gesture as Prokopchuk sat down. Next to stand up was John Myerson. "Our group worked on engagement. Our starting premise was that there is a correlation between two unfortunate Gallup findings: first, that most people are either not engaged or are actively disengaged in their work; and second, that most people feel their greatest strengths are not being called upon in their jobs. We really liked Carol Jean's idea of a 'fill-in-the-blank' job description. The details obviously have to be worked out with HR, but the idea would be that anyone could complete an application telling us how they could deploy something they love to do, but which is not part of their formal job description, to help us better serve our community. I love Carol Jean's example of the nurse who wrote poems for her patients, even though it wasn't part of her job description. We all agreed that if people felt like even a small part of their daily work was doing something they love to do, something they had personally designed, they would be more engaged in their jobs and in the mission of Memorial Medical Center."

Myerson looked up at Carol Jean, smiled and shrugged. "Good poets borrow and great poets steal. Right?" Then he looked around the room. "After college, I went off to graduate school. My best friend joined a rock band and hit the road in a secondhand school bus. I thought he was nuts. Today he lives in Beverly Hills and drives a Ferrari. If just ten percent of our people could apply just ten percent of their time doing something about which they are unstoppably passionate, like writing poetry for patients, I think we could end up with the most engaged and committed workforce of any hospital in America. Malinda, do you want to add anything?"

> We need to be more efficient in systems and operations so that there is more time for the things that really matter, like compassion and listening.

Malinda St. John was director of medical nursing and reported to Martinez. She was part of Myerson's group. "Yes, I do," she said as she stood up. "Carol Jean has been making the point that compassion is one of our core values and productivity is not, but that observing our management priorities you might think it was the other way around. One of the things we discussed in our group was how to solve this dilemma with the *genius of AND* and not get trapped in the *tyranny of OR*. In order to be truly engaged, people need the time to really listen to patients and coworkers, and listening is at the heart of compassion. But in today's world, we cannot afford to sacrifice productivity. Our group's conclusion was that we need to become evermore efficient in our systems to free a people's time for the things that really matter, like listening. That also means," she said with a little wave to Dale Prokopchuk, "long-term job security for the members of QILT."

"I couldn't agree more," said Carol Jean. "And it gets back to what I keep saying about the left brain counts but the right brain matters: to be a great organization, you have to both count and matter. Okay, who wants to go next?"

Molly Anderson, the director of human resources, stood up next. "Our group focused on belonging. We frankly don't do a very good job of making our people feel like partners. We came up with two specific recommendations. First, our current employee newsletter reads more like a society column than a report to owners. We think that every month our MMC caregiving partners – Linda, we love that title – deserve a detailed and understandable report on the organization's finances, operations, and the chief concerns of the leadership team. Our second recommendation is that we all do a better job of conducting meaningful staff meetings in our own areas, and that on our rounds we make a point of proactively talking about why we need our caregiving partners to help us move our results on productivity and patient satisfaction in the right direction. Of course, this means that most of us are going to have to do a better job of understanding these things ourselves. And do a better job of getting out of our offices and putting our feet on the street. Any questions?"

No one had questions, so Anderson took her seat again. Without waiting to be called upon Cassandra Wilkinson, director of environmental services, stood up and said, "I'll go next. Our group talked about passion. We actually think the best way to get people to be more passionate about their work here is to make sure they're having fun. If we're having fun we'll be more, not less, productive. We were intrigued by what Carol Jean told us about the power of rituals to reinforce culture. So we put together a list of a dozen possible rituals." Wilkinson held up a pad filled with scribbled notes. "I'm not going to read all of them, but here are two. First, what if once a month we members of the leadership team were to station ourselves at each entry on each shift to welcome our caregiving partners with a candy bar as they came on duty? Like maybe a Payday in April when we pay our taxes, or a Sugar Daddy in June for Father's Day. Wouldn't that send a message that we really do care?" she asked, pointing to the WE CARE banner on the wall.

"The second ritual is that we teach everyone how to do the MMC Roar, as my colleague Justin Demaray will now demonstrate." Demaray was from the corporate materials management office, and known for his irreverent sense of humor. He stood up, clenched his arms in front of him professional wrestler style, and let out a king-of-the-jungle roar. He sat down to great applause and Wilkinson continued. "We'd like to see every shift on every unit begin with a group roar. At first, people are going to think we're crazy. In fact," she said with a laugh, "some people already do think we're crazy. But just look at Justin. Doesn't he look like he's ready to go to work and that nothing's going to get in his way?" Demaray stood and did another Hulk Hogan pose. "We're hoping that the rest of you will give us some more suggestions – the wackier the better."

Wilkinson started to sit down, then quickly stood up again. "One more thing. We all agreed that we need to resume the employee picnic that got axed in budget cuts five years ago. It was a wonderful ritual, and people still miss it." Myerson cocked his head and scrunched his lips upon hearing this. It was news to him that there ever had been an employee picnic, much less that it had fallen under the budget ax.

"Very good," Carol Jean said, choosing to move quickly over the picnic issue. "And speaking of initiative, who's going to take the initiative to report from the group that worked on that cultural characteristic?"

Sarah slowly rose from her chair in the back of the room. "For those who don't know me, I'm Sarah Rutledge from pediatric oncology. I'm filling in for Amanda today because she's out of town. My group covered initiative, and they took the initiative to tell me to take notes. We all agreed that we have a lot of work to do on this one. Jerry Patterson…" Sarah nodded to Patterson, who was the administrative director for all of MMC's mental health programs, "explained the concept of 'learned helplessness' to us, and we agreed that it's something we need to deal with here at MMC. Too many people think they can't take action without management go-ahead, then management waits downstairs wondering why people don't take action. There's a serious disconnect here. Owners don't sit around waiting for someone to tell them to mow their lawns or check the oil in their cars, but lots of our employees – I'm sorry, I mean our caregiving partners – just walk by problems they don't want to own. We need a mind shift, that encourages people on the front lines to take the initiative when something needs to be done.

And they need to be supported in taking initiative by their managers and supervisors."

Sarah looked up at Carol Jean and shrugged as if to say *I can't believe I'm hearing myself say this.* "Carol Jean told us that Florence Nightingale's attitude about getting things done was sort of 'proceed until apprehended.' Well, we think that should become official MMC policy – if a caregiving partner sees something that needs to be done, whatever it is, they should take the initiative to start getting it done. But since we tried something like that in Nursing and it didn't really work, we need to help people feel more personally empowered. So we think we should take *The Self-Empowerment Pledge* and share it with everyone at MMC. Maybe by making laminated cards that can go on our lanyards or something. But the emphasis should be on how those seven promises can help us in our personal lives, like managing time and money or being a better parent. If people buy into self-empowerment at home, then that power will follow them to work. We also need a recognition and reward program of some sort, at least until the new behaviors are in place. Jerry," she said, looking over at Patterson sitting at the next table, "you want to tell them what we had in mind?"

"Sure," Patterson said, standing up as Sarah sat down, a palpable look of relief on her face. "This is not going to be any sort of quick fix. We're talking about some pretty significant changes in behavior, meaning that there must also be changes in underlying beliefs, assumptions and attitudes. 'Proceed until apprehended' has a nice ring to it, though it might be too big a step for now. But we thought about riffing on the 'better to ask forgiveness than permission' theme with a program we'd call 'Permission Granted.' It needs work – and everyone in our group has agreed to keep working on it – but we'd see a three-step process. First, define the areas where people have permission *in advance* to take action – for example, helping a patient or saving the organization money. Second, define a range of the sorts of actions that are included, say leaving the nursing unit for 30 minutes to make a trip to Dairy Queen because Timmy Mallory has a craving for a Dilly Bar." Sarah smiled, held one thumb in the air and pointed the other thumb to her chest to indicate that she would volunteer for the mission.

"And finally," Patterson continued, "specifying some form of recognition and reward for people who do take initiative on these things. Now, I know there is some resistance to rewarding people for doing something they should be doing anyway, and I share that sentiment. But realistically we've got to acknowledge that, like Zig Ziglar says, everyone listens to the same radio station – WIIFM, or 'What's In It For Me?' A formal recognition program will also help us track how well we're doing. In fact, while there will probably be some upfront expense, we think that over time this will actually save money, because if people really think and act like owners, they'll help us find ways to cut costs and be more efficient."

"Whew," Carol Jean exclaimed as Patterson took his seat, "this group is thinking big. 'Permission Granted.' That is an incredible concept. I think you're right about the problem of learned helplessness, and it's not just here at MMC. I see symptoms at every client I've worked with. Now, given today's concerns about healthcare costs, effective stewardship of resources is more important than ever. Who's going to speak for that group?"

Heidi Buckner was director of materials management and one of the newest members of the management team, having recently come from a large hospital in Pittsburgh. To no one's surprise, she had immediately gravitated toward the stewardship group, and been delegated to be that group's spokesperson. "First of all, while our group understands Carol Jean's comment about how the word 'accountability' has taken on lots of negative connotations, we do believe that effective stewardship begins with accountability, and that even though it's one of our core values here at MMC, we don't do a very good job of holding ourselves accountable – including for the ways that we utilize resources. So our first recommendation is that we establish four person accountability groups within the management team, with the expectation that they routinely meet to review each member's goals and current progress, and to pitch in and help anyone who is getting behind on their goals to get caught up."

Carol Jean smiled inwardly as she noticed how many people were nodding from the neck up and squirming from the neck down. "Our second recommendation," Buckner continued, "is that we do a much better job of telling our people what's at stake if we aren't a cost leader. If a real crunch comes, programs like hospice, the drug treatment center, and the subsidy for employee gym memberships could be in jeopardy. People need a bigger reason than the boss telling them to do more with less if we really want them to buy into being a part of the cost control solution. And our third recommendation is that we ask patients to tell us how *they* think we could reduce our costs. You know, we get lots of letters complaining about hospital bills – people who think we're really charging them twelve dollars for an aspirin and things like that. So in every patient admission packet, why don't we include something that says we're serious about reducing healthcare costs here at MMC, and if they see something we could do better, we'd like to hear from them."

Carol Jean joined in the applause as Buckner took her seat. "Thanks Heidi and group, for those great ideas. I especially like your third recommendation, which I think could actually expand the sense of ownership to patients and to the larger community." Carol Jean smiled at Wendy Harper who, she noticed, had been a part of Heidi's group. "If we can do all of the things we've talked about thus far, I think there's going to be a great deal of pride in this medical center. Who's going to report for the group that worked on the pride characteristic?"

"That will be me," Dr. Franklin said, taking his feet. Some of the people in the room had never seen him wearing anything but his long white lab coat, but today he was in a cardigan sweater. "I think most of you know that I have volunteered to chair a workgroup looking at how we can do more to honor the dignity of each person who works at, and is cared for by, Memorial Medical Center. That work is integrally related to the pride we each feel in our jobs, our professions, and our hospital. Carol Jean has pointed out how profoundly the answer one gives to the simple icebreaker question 'what do you do?' will forever influence the perceptions of the person asking the question. So we think, and I'm serious about this, that each of us as leaders should help our people come up with a creative way to answer that question which forestalls that sort of judgment. An answer that, instead of sounding almost apologetic, conveys pride." Franklin placed a closed fist on his chest for emphasis. "An answer that conveys this: 'I love what I do, I'm good at what I do, and what I do is important.' And some variation of that should be our common response."

Out of habit, Dr. Franklin reached with both hands for the stethoscope that was always around his neck, and instead settled for holding onto the collars of his sweater. "But it's not enough to just teach people the words. If we really do care, we need to help people cultivate an underlying positive self-image and high self-esteem. As Cassandra pointed out, some people will think it's ridiculous, but our group believes it's imperative. I've been thinking a lot about something Carol Jean said to me in our first meeting, that the non-negotiable first step in building a winning team is coaching each of the team's players to see themselves as winners in the game of life. At one time, I might have said this is something which cannot be taught. I now believe, and here I'm speaking for our entire group, that it not only can be taught, if we want to become the great organization we keep talking about being, then it must be taught."

> Some people aren't going to buy in to a culture of ownership and a few will actively seek to sabotage the effort. Are you willing to raise your expectations, lower your tolerance level for deviation from those expectations, and perhaps lose some people who have good technical skills but a bad attitude?

Dr. Franklin sat down to more applause, and Carol Jean walked out to the front of the stage. "Thank you all. I'm impressed! You've obviously put a great deal of thought into your deliberations, and if we carry through with all of this we'll see impressive changes in the organization. Before we break for lunch, though, I have two questions. First, as several of you have already alluded, some people just aren't going to buy in to this culture of ownership. And there will be a few who actively seek to sabotage the effort. So the question is, are you willing to raise your expectations, lower your tolerance level for deviation from those expectations, and perhaps lose some people who have good technical skills but a bad attitude?"

Molly Anderson spoke up first. "I don't think we have a choice. Obviously, we want to do everything we can to gain buy-in, but I don't think we should put up with toxic resistance to change. I'd add one more thing, though, and that is we need to communicate very clearly what we're doing and why, and not rush things. If we do all the things we've talked about this morning, it's going to be quite a shock to the system. I think we need that shock, but not all at once." There were assenting nods all around the room.

"Excellent points, Molly. Now here's my second question: making the investment to move from a culture of accountability toward a culture of ownership is going to cost some money. To start something up only to shut it down when the budget gets tight, the way the employee picnic evidently got cut, will be worse than doing nothing at all. Are we willing to make building a culture of ownership an operational priority, and not just a good intention?"

Terry Barnes, the chief financial officer, raised his hand. "I was on the group looking at pride with Dr. Franklin. Some of the things we talked about *will* cost money, and that money is not currently in the budget. I didn't even mention that during our discussions, though. If something is sufficiently important to us as an organization, we will find the money to do it. Put another way," he said as he did a quick scan around the room, then fixed his eyes upon Linda Martinez, "I don't want to hear any of you blaming me and the finance department for a failure to move ahead on any of this. If you have the creativity to come up with great ideas, and the courage to act upon those ideas, we will find a way to pay for them. I've been convinced that fostering a culture of ownership is an investment, not just an expense. It's our collective job to make sure that we gain a great return on that investment. And not just in monetary terms, but also in people terms."

"Thanks Terry," Carol Jean said. "I think you all should be very proud of the work you've done this morning. It's almost noon, and they've prepared a nice lunch for us out on the patio, so let's break for now – but I hope these great discussions will continue over the lunch tables." She started for the patio, then noticed that Sarah was still sitting at her table in the back of the room, alone and writing furiously.

"What are you working on?" Looked over Sarah's shoulder at the scribbled notes covering the pad on the table, and couldn't make out a single word. "Did you take a special handwriting class at the medical school?"

Sarah laughed and turned the pad over to be face-down on the table. "My group asked me to be our official recorder, and I want to get my notes organized while it's all still fresh in my head."

"I'm impressed," Carol Jean said as she pulled up a chair. "You're really taking this seriously."

Sarah shrugged and grinned. "Now that I'm part of the conspiracy, I want to do my part."

"So what are your impressions – as the newest member of the conspiracy? And what do the other nurses in your Monday morning group think of this new Sarah Rutledge?"

Sarah took a slow deep breath before she answered. "I'd love to be able to tell you that they all like the new me, but I can't. Not yet, anyway. Some of them think it's great. Anna asked me what drugs I've been taking because she wants to start taking them too. I told her The Florence Prescription. Some of the others are pretty negative about it. One person, someone I've always considered a real friend, accused me of selling out to the suits. But I don't really care about that, because what really matters is that I like the new me."

Carol Jean smiled and shook her head. "This is not the new you, Sarah, this is the real you."

"Yeah, it sure feels more real. Not necessarily easy – but real."

"It's going to take a while, perhaps a long while. But imagine how much nicer it will be, coming to work every day and not having to be infected by someone else's toxic emotional negativity."

Sarah slowly stretched her arms and legs and arched her back, reminding Carol Jean of a cat who's just eaten and is now looking for a warm patch of sunshine. "Yeah, that will be nice. But there's another problem."

"What's that?"

"The people in this room. Today it's all warm and fuzzy, but some of these managers aren't going to buy-in to this culture of ownership. Oh, they'll say all the right words – you know, empowerment and accountability and ownership – but at the end of the day they're not going to give up trying to manage people by controlling them, no matter what John Myerson or anyone else says."

Carol Jean nodded thoughtfully. "You're right, of course. As Florence says, the bigger the change, the more entrenched the resistance. Cultural transformation always follows the snowball principle."

"What's that?"

"If you set a snowball on the ground at the top of a hill, nothing happens until you give it a push. It rolls an inch or two, then you have to give it another push, then another. It takes a lot of pushing, but eventually the snowball gets big enough, and has enough momentum, that nothing can stop it."

"Yeah, but you've got to have a long enough hill."

"Don't worry about that. We have a long enough hill. Now let's go eat."

After lunch, Carol Jean had each group spend another two hours working out details for their ideas. Then she brought the whole group together to outline a master timetable for communicating and implementing the various elements of their plan. That evening, she went out to dinner with John Myerson, Linda Martinez, and Terry Barnes. They were excited about moving ahead, but (with good reason, she told them) apprehensive about the likely resistance and gaining staff buy-in. "I'll tell you what," Carol Jean had said, "when we figure that one out, I'll make it the subject of my next book. And I'll credit MMC in the acknowledgments."

Back in her hotel room, Carol Jean set her iPod to play her favorite Mozart piano concerto, the twentieth, which she loved partly because it was a great metaphor for much of life, the way it begins on such an ominous note and concludes with cheerful optimism. Then she settled in on the sofa to read a good book. She'd hoped that Florence would show up, or that Sarah would call, but instead woke up sometime after midnight with a stiff neck and her book on the floor. As she walked over to the bed, the whimsical thought struck her that Florence and Sarah had gone out together for a nightcap.

CHAPTER SIXTEEN

It had been nearly three months since Carol Jean had submitted her final report to John Myerson at Memorial Medical Center. Today she'd spent the day meeting with the leadership team of a new client hospital in Chicago. After barely touching a hotel room service dinner, she'd settled in on the sofa to read yet another report on the crisis in healthcare capital financing. "One more healthcare crisis" she muttered as she scanned the pages. But she couldn't concentrate. She couldn't get her mind off the email she'd received from Sarah Rutledge the day before, and the phone call she'd gotten from John Myerson that morning confirming what Sarah had told her. Timmy Mallory – Florence's brave little soldier – had slipped into a coma two days ago. They didn't expect him to come out of it. She drifted off to sleep on the sofa, with fire-breathing dragons populating her dreams.

"Wake up, Carol Jean, wake up." Carol Jean's spastic reaction to the nudging of her shoulder almost caused her to fall on the floor.

"What is it? What time is it?" Carol Jean struggled up to a sitting position. Nightingale was standing beside the sofa, an urgent look on her face. She appeared considerably older than the last time Carol Jean had seen her three months earlier. "Hurry," she implored, tugging on Carol Jean's sleeve. "There's something you need to see."

Carol Jean tried to clear away the cobwebs of sleep, "What is it?" But instead of hearing an answer, she found herself standing side-by-side with Nightingale outside the door of a hospital room. She tried again to rub the sleep out of her eyes, then looked at the sign next to the door. Room 819. Timmy Mallory's room at Memorial Medical Center. Her heart skipped a beat. The door was open just wide enough for the two of them to enter, Carol Jean tracing Nightingale's footsteps.

Carol Jean recognized Patty Mallory, a nurse from the MMC Emergency Department, standing by Timmy's bed. She'd known that Timmy's mom was an E.D. nurse, and had seen her from afar, but they'd never met. Then Carol Jean saw the little girl with the gap-toothed smile she'd met down at the fountain. The little girl who'd said that her big brother was in the hospital, and who'd offered to take Carol Jean home with her if she was homeless. The little girl who shared Carol Jean's belief in the reality of invisible friends. She was perched on the side of her brother's bed, holding his hand. Though Patty had not seemed to notice their entering the room, the little girl looked up and smiled at Florence and Carol Jean. Then she returned her attention to her big brother.

Nightingale stepped over to the bedside. "Hello Audrey, how's our brave little soldier tonight?" Patty again took no notice, but the little girl put a forefinger to her lips and whispered, "Shh – he's sleeping." Carol Jean noticed the sword that Myerson had given Timmy was laid out on the bed next to him. The little boy looked so frail, Carol Jean wondered if he had already died.

"Don't you think it's time for him to wake up?" Nightingale smiled at the little girl as though Audrey was the daughter she'd never had herself.

Audrey nodded emphatically, looking suddenly very solemn. She leaned close to her brother's ear. "Timmy, Timmy. Time to wake up. Wake up, Timmy."

Patty, still oblivious to the presence of Carol Jean and Florence, put a hand on Audrey's head. Her lower lip quivered and she fought back the tears that had already established a well-marked path down her cheeks. "Honey, I don't think... Let's let him sleep a while longer. Okay?"

Ignoring her mother, Audrey gently shook Timmy by the shoulders.

"Timmy, time to wake up." Then she kissed him on the forehead.

Timmy's body rocked as though an electric shock had passed through him. His eyes opened, then closed again. "Timmy…" Audrey said, more insistently than before, "Time to wake up, Timmy." She again shook him by the shoulders, but this time there was no reaction. She picked out several ice chips from the pitcher on the over-bed table and moistened Timmy's lips, the way the nurses had showed her. "Wake up, Timmy." Audrey picked out a few more ice chips and resumed the ritual. "Time to wake up," she cooed.

Time to wake up! Carol Jean awoke with a start to the crescendoing final movement of Beethoven's ninth symphony, which was the ringtone on her cell phone. She almost fell on her face trying to make the leap from the couch to the coffee table in a near-panicked attempt to get to it before it stopped ringing. She started to answer but her voice cracked and she tried again. "Hello, this is Carol Jean Hawtrey."

Carol Jean could hear voices in the background, but at first no one spoke to her. "Just a minute, I'll be right there," she heard a familiar voice shouting at what sounded like an arm's length from the phone. Then, evidently now speaking into the phone's mouthpiece, the caller spoke with breathless urgency. "Carol Jean, it's Sarah Rutledge from Memorial Medical Center. Sorry to be calling so late, but I knew you'd want to know."

Now Carol Jean remembered her dream, and in her mind could still hear the voice of little Audrey Mallory. *Wake up, Timmy, it's time to wake up.* She felt a sickening clench in the pit of her stomach.

"No problem, Sarah, I wasn't asleep."

"You're still not a very good liar, Carol Jean," Sarah said. Carol Jean heard more commotion in the background and heard Sarah holler, "Okay, I'll be right there. Hang on!"

"Are you at a bar, Sarah?"

"No, not yet. Listen, Carol Jean, Timmy Mallory…" Sarah paused and Carol Jean's heart raced as she braced herself for the news. "You're not going to believe it, Carol Jean. Timmy Mallory is awake. Oh my God, it's a miracle. We never thought… But he's awake. He asked for you. I told him you weren't here, and he told me to tell you he's back in the dragon-slaying business. Then he asked me to call down to the kitchen and order up some tacos and a milkshake. This is a miracle!" There was more commotion in the background. "Listen, I gotta go. I'll call you tomorrow." Before the line clicked off Carol Jean heard Sarah shouting, "You put that sword down, young man, and get back into bed this minute!"

Carol Jean fell back onto the sofa, not sure whether to laugh or cry, and ended up doing both.

In her mind's eye, Carol Jean saw Timmy Mallory running down the hospital corridor, dragging his IV pole with one hand and waving his sword with the other, proclaiming to all within earshot that Sir Timothy the Dragonslayer had returned to the battle, wounded but determined to prevail in the end.

That was the ultimate meaning of the Florence Prescription, she thought. All the pre-program planning, the leadership retreats and staff training, all the consultant reports and coaching, were geared toward this one goal: to foster a culture of ownership that honors victory of the spirit as much as it celebrates healing of the body. A culture that honors Sarah Rutledge for sitting at the bedside of her patient singing a lullaby after the end of her shift. A culture that honors Jerry Rathman for fighting to keep open his drug and alcohol unit because the community needed it. A culture that honors Carlos the housekeeper for dancing with his mop in the corridor. A culture that honors Linda Martinez for taking her nurse managers offsite to learn the skills of self-empowerment. A culture that honors John Myerson and Bill Bristow for looking at each other and seeing people, not just figures at the bargaining table. A culture that honors little Timmy Mallory for fighting dragons with his imagination that the doctors could not kill with their technology. A culture of ownership where investing in people takes precedence over investing in buildings.

Carol Jean put aside any thoughts she might have had about going to bed, even though it was almost midnight. She walked over to the desk and pushed aside all the notes she'd been making for the report she was working on for her client. Tonight she had something more important to write: a letter to Sir Timothy Mallory, the Dragonslayer of Memorial Medical Center.

Epilog

On this day 200 years ago, Florence Nightingale led a small band of nurses to Turkey to care for British casualties of the Crimean war.

- The London Times, November 4, 2054, page 14

It was as she would have wanted it. There were no crowds, no brass bands playing God Save the Queen, no speeches. Just a gentle wind playing across the grounds of St. Margaret Church in East Wellow, England, the final resting place of Miss Florence Nightingale.

The man who had come so far now stopped twenty feet from the small and simple obelisk that marked her grave. He leaned on a walking cane with his right hand. In his left, he held two roses, one red and one pink. The wind rippled his thinning hair as he slowly paced the final steps toward the tombstone, the way someone might walk down the aisle of a church preparing to receive Communion.

Upon reaching the grave, the man leaned more heavily on his cane as he bent to one knee. If you'd been watching from afar, you would have thought he was carrying on a conversation with someone, though he himself was the only person visible on the grounds that morning.

The man laid his flowers, pink and red, against the gravestone and said goodbye. Then he pulled himself up with his cane and walked slowly back the way he'd come. There were still dragons to slay, and Dr. Timothy Mallory needed to return to the battle. His brave little soldiers were depending on him.

The End

Bibliography

For more on the life and work of Florence Nightingale, we encourage you to read:

Bostridge, Mark. *Florence Nightingale: The Making of an Icon.* New York: Farrar, Straus and Giroux, 2008.

Dossey, Barbara Montgomery. *Florence Nightingale: Mystic, Visionary, Healer.* Springhouse PA: Springhouse Corporation, 2000.

Dossey, Barbara Montgomery; Selanders, Louise C.; Beck, Deva-Marie; Attewell, Alex. *Florence Nightingale Today: Healing, Leadership, Global Action.* Silver Spring MD: American Nurses Association, 2005.

Gill, Gillian. *Nightingales: The Extraordinary Upbringing and Curious Life of Miss Florence Nightingale.* New York: Random House Trade Publications, 2004.

Nightingale, Florence: *Notes on Nursing: What It Is, and What It Is Not.* New York: Dover Publications, 1969.

Small, Hugh. *Florence Nightingale: Avenging Angel.* New York: St. Martin's Press, 1998.

Webb, Val. *Florence Nightingale: The Making of a Radical Theologian.* St. Louis, MO: Chalice Press, 2002.

There is a wonderful website tribute to Florence Nightingale established by Country Joe (of Country Joe and the Fish fame) at **http://www.countryjoe.com/nightingale/**.

Learn about *The Nightingale Initiative of Global Health* and sign the Nightingale Declaration at **http://www.nightingaledeclaration.net/**.

Learn about *The Nightingale Moment* at the website of the American Holistic Nurses Association: **http://www.ahna.org/**.

Acknowledgments

This book has been ten years in the making, and reflects the journey we ourselves have been following at Values Coach. Our original focus on teaching values-based life and leadership skills in the organizational setting has led us to a much deeper understanding of how organizations change – they don't. People change. We are deeply in debt to our client organizations, from whom we have learned so much and whose leaders are such an inspiration to us.

Patrick Charmel and the team at Griffin Hospital, which for the past ten years has been one of Fortune magazine's *100 Best Companies to Work For* (an unparalleled achievement for a hospital) truly are changing the face of healthcare. In 1999, they were one of the first hospitals to adopt the Values Coach course on *The Twelve Core Action Values* as the core curriculum for their Dare to Care program, and their early influence on the direction of the course endures to this day.

More than any other organization, the Planetree Alliance has picked up the torch for patient-centered care that was originally lit by Florence Nightingale. It's been our privilege to work with more than a dozen Planetree hospitals, and each year Values Coach is proud to sponsor the bookstore at the annual Planetree conference. We believe that every hospital in the world should be a member. Susan Frampton, Randy Carter, Lisa Donnarumma, Kit Alff, Marie Sullivan, Michael Rosen, the rest of the Planetree staff and Planetree coordinators and administrators in hospitals around the world are carrying on the Nightingale tradition. The late Laura Gilpin was a kindred spirit with Florence Nightingale, and her poetry is a lasting legacy.

The philosophy in this book has been profoundly influenced by our longstanding client Auto-Owners Insurance, a Fortune 500 company from which every hospital could learn lessons about building a culture of ownership. Chairman Roger Looyenga, CEO Ron Simon, President

Jeff Harrold and the 3,400 associates who make up the No Problem People® team at Auto-Owners are a shining example of a business that is successful because of its commitment and adherence to core values. Jeff Stroburg and the team at West Central, one of America's most innovative agricultural cooperatives and sponsor of the world's largest producer of biodiesel, have proven that a small Iowa town can be the hub for a growing worldwide business. In particular, we are perpetually amazed by the creative genius of Sarah Dorman (thanks for the candy bar idea!). Shoemaker-Haaland Professional Engineers has taken cultural transformation seriously even as they go through the biggest transition in the history of the company.

Over the years, it has been our good fortune to work with many hospitals and other healthcare organizations that have greatly influenced our thinking. It has been a joy and a privilege to work with leaders (and the teams that support them) like Pat Charmel, Todd Linden, Fran Finley, Judy Rich (who taught us about the power of feet on the street), Ryan Smith, Dave Gilbreath, Jeff Hill, Sandy Haryasz, Alex Spector, Les Donahue, Don Currier, Mimi Roberson, Genny Maroc, Paul Cox, Don Patterson, Ed Lamb, Charlie Franz, Heidi Gil, Dennis Smith, Tim Barrett, Donna Katen-Bahensky, Kelley Kieffer, Brian Hoefle, Dave McClung, Thom Greenlaw (the inspiration behind Carlos), Charlie Collins, Sharon Hayes, Terrie Long, Linda Shearer, Phil Feisal, Dr. Ray Troiano, Leigh Cox, Dr. Ellen Cram, John Denbo, Frank Lazzaro, Jeanne Locklear, Kathleen Allman, Ron Muecke, Rand Wortman, Jim Kineer, Becki Benoit, Art Spies, Cristine Henry, Deona Ryan, Ed Barr, Dr. Jim Blagg, Jody Monk, Margaret Greenly, Lorraine Robertson, Cindy Toth, Rod Betit, Patricia Read, Brian Shantz, and many others.

We also wish to acknowledge the support and encouragement of the staff at the American Hospital Association, and especially Alden Solovy, Laura Woodburn, Connie Lang, Jane Jeffries, Rick Hill, Dave Parlin, Patti Costello, Cathy Sewell, and Stephanie Drake. Chuck Lauer has been a great friend and supporter of the Values Coach mission, and we are grateful for his leadership in the healthcare industry, and for the wonderful foreword he provided for this book. Kim Schultz at

Amazing Mail has been a friend and supporter from the start.

Early reviewers of the manuscript contributed critiques and suggestions that have made this a better book. It is painful for us to go back and read through the early drafts of this work, so we have true appreciation for Joy Moore, Todd Linden, Steven Tye, Mark Newton, Fran Finley, Sally Mathis Hartwig, Ron Reed, Dr. Ralph Bovard, Ann Younger Crandall, Jack Durbin, Jeanine Sedlacek, Jonna Scott-Blakes, Kathleen Cretier, Kathleen Allman, Laura Wynohrad, Mark Cotter, Roger Looyenga, Ken Gomez, Patty Haggard, Peter Cohen, Duane Rossmann, Doug Wakefield, Robert Boulware, Gymbeaux Brown, Susan Collins, Wendy Tabellion, Barb Kalm, and others who took the time to read and comment.

We appreciate the support, ideas, and referrals that come to us from the Values Coach Advisory Board, whose members include Larry Prybil, Chuck Peters, Chris Atchison, Lisa Bluder, Mollie Marti, Ted Garnett, Roger Looyenga, Steven Tye, and Susan Frampton. Advisory Board member Dave Altman, Executive Vice President for Research, Innovation & Product Development at the Center for Creative Leadership, has been a friend and supporter since the days he and Joe worked together trying to stop the white collar drug pushers at big tobacco from hooking our children on their addictive and deadly products, and has been a supporter of Values Coach from the day our doors opened fifteen years ago.

Kurt Stocker, Elena Barabashova and Hung Viet Tran help keep us connected in cyberspace. Lisa Peterson and the graphic design crew at Studio 6 Sense were a joy to work with in creating this book. Annette Ridenour and her team at Aesthetics Inc. and David Corbin and Melanie Rivera at Audio Aesthetics inspire us to think beautiful. Scott Meador and the Sunday study group keep us humble. To Father Michael Crosby, thank you for reminding us to Thank God Ahead of Time.

Thousands of *Spark Plug* readers and Values Coach Connect members from around the world, many of whom are healthcare professionals (or as Linda Martinez calls them in our book, caregiving partners), keep us inspired.

Special thanks to the speakers bureaus that have helped us spread the Values Coach message including AHA Health Forum Faculty, Healthcare Speakers Network, Five Star Speakers and Trainers, BigSpeak!, Midwest Speakers Bureau, Otellus, the Anne Land Agency, JW Speakers Bureau, Walters International Speakers Bureau, Speak Inc., American Program Bureau, Business Speakers Bureau, and Eagles Talent Connection. Special appreciation to all of you meeting planners who do all the work to make things work, but too rarely stand under the lights.

From Joe: Thanks to Dick for being a coach, colleague and role model for the past ten years. Thanks to Michael Ray and Jeffrey Pfeffer, professors at the Stanford Graduate School of Business, for the lasting influence on my ideas about creativity and leadership. Thanks to Mom and Dad for their love and support through every roll of the roller coaster, brothers Steven the tycoon and Allen the can man, Sister Nancy the globetrotting scholar, daughter Annie the future Nobel Prize winning medical researcher, and son Doug the brilliant PhD candidate. Joe also gives a flap of the wings to Larry the Motivational Bird for making him laugh and reminding him to sing. But above all, this book is dedicated to Sally, Miss Bonkers, without whom none of it would be possible. Happiness is being married to your best friend!

From Dick: Thanks to Joe for being so passionately persistent in his pursuit of sharing his knowledge of values-based living. Thanks to all the people in my life who serve as models living their values every day in all they do.

Study Questions for
The Florence Prescription

These questions will help you think about how the lessons of *The Florence Prescription* can apply in your hospital, and in your own life. Contemplating your answers, and discussing them with groups within the hospital, will help you make the most of the book.

How does your organization do on the eight essential characteristics of a culture of ownership? How would you rate your hospital on the eight essential characteristics of a culture of ownership that were outlined by Carol Jean Hawtrey in this story: Commitment, Engagement, Passion, Initiative, Stewardship, Belonging, Fellowship, and Pride? How about your own behavior and that of your immediate coworkers? What do you think Carol Jean would say to your hospital CEO if she were to consult with your organization?

How high are your silo walls and how can you bring them down? Carol Jean told MMC board member Wendy Harper that her next book was going to be about creating a greater spirit of community within hospitals by bringing down the silo walls that separate departments – and that separate people from each other. One of her key recommendations to CEO John Myerson was that managers spend less time in their offices and more time out speaking with people. Dale Prokopchuk told leadership retreat participants that his group worked on the characteristic of Fellowship, and recommended fostering a support group culture as a way of lowering silo walls. What actions could bring down the silo walls and create a greater spirit of community in your organization?

Are you who you say you are? Just as a fish is oblivious to the water in which it swims or a bird never notices the air under its wings, we can become so used to our workplace environments that we don't even notice how negative and toxic they would appear to an outside observer. We might use words such as *caring, nurturing, compassionate* and *empowering* to describe what we think of the cultural climate we think we are cultivating, but based upon objective observations of our actual behaviors, the proverbial Man from Mars might instead use words like *critical, self-pitying,* and *disempowered.*

What is the emotional climate of your hospital? The environment of our hospitals is more than just the physical space in which we work. It's also the emotional climate we create. While the physical environment is important for making a good first impression, the emotional climate is more likely to influence patient perceptions of clinical quality and human compassion, and more likely to determine loyalty and longevity of good people. How would you describe the emotional climate of your organization? In what ways could it be enhanced?

How are your attitudes affecting your patients? Emotions, both positive and negative, are contagious. For most patients, hospitals are already a frightening place to be. If the organizational culture is characterized by negative attitudes (as reflected in the prevalence of criticizing, complaining, and rumor-mongering), we can actually be contributing to iatrogenic anxiety and depression on the part of our patients. Do you really provide patients with a healing environment? What can you do in your hospital to create a shared vision of being a healing environment that is free of toxic (and contagious) emotional negativity? If everyone in your hospital were to stop criticizing, complaining, and gossiping, how much more time would there be for direct patient care and all of the other things that people complain they never have time for? And if people were to take that commitment home with them, how much more pleasant and nurturing with their home lives be?

Does your hospital allow mud to be spattered on people's souls? When Sarah Rutledge listened to two other nurses gossiping (actually, spreading lies) about a third nurse, she said she felt like her soul had been spattered with mud. Hospitals are notorious for their rumor mills, but as Lori Palatnik and Bob Burg point out in their book *Gossip: Ten*

Pathways to Eliminate It from Your Life and Transform Your Soul, this practice harms everyone involved (especially, the authors say, passive listeners), and it contributes to a more negative and toxic cultural climate within the organization. What actions can your hospital leadership take to promote a more free flow of accurate information so as to more quickly counter rumors? What changes can all staff make to foster a culture that is intolerant of this unethical behavior?

Do we empower caregivers to empower patients? A fundamental quality of patient-centered care is empowering patients to be active participants in their healing, and not just passive recipients of our care. But before caregivers can help patients feel empowered, they must feel that they themselves are empowered to do so. If the people within your organization would hold themselves accountable for living the seven promises of *The Self- Empowerment Pledge* that Carol Jean presented to the nursing leadership retreat at Memorial Medical Center, how much more empowered would they feel? How much more effective would they be at empowering patients? What actions can you take to disseminate and promote this pledge?

Do we empower or do we apprehend? "Proceed until apprehended." That's how Carol Jean described the Nightingale philosophy of putting patients first. How would that philosophy fit into the culture of your hospital? Would a nurse in your hospital find the time (or rather, make the time) to sing to a little boy who at that moment needed a song more than he needed pills? Or would she be "apprehended" by a manager more concerned about meeting budget targets than meeting patient needs? In their book *Built to Last*, Jim Collins and Jerry Porras wrote that great companies replace "the tyranny of OR" with "the genius of AND." What actions can we take to move from the tyranny of productivity OR patient caring to the genius of productivity AND patient caring?

Who answers patient call lights? When no one answered Timmy's call light, Florence Nightingale said, "We must do better than this." The fact is that anyone can see a patient's call light on and walk into the room. They might be able to take care of the problem if it's something as simple as refilling a water pitcher, but at the very least they can reassure the patient that their nurse will be coming, and in the process help to take a bit of pressure off the nurse. What more can you do to foster a culture in which everyone feels empowered to "answer patient call lights" – or take any other actions that help you serve patients, support each other, and best utilize resources in your hospital?

About the Authors

oe Tye is CEO and Head Coach of Values Coach Inc. He earned a masters degree in hospital and health administration from The University of Iowa and an MBA from the Stanford Graduate School of Business, where he was class co-president. Prior to founding Values Coach in 1994, he was chief operating officer for a 750-bed community teaching hospital. Joe was founding president of the Association of Air Medical Services, and was a leader in the campaign to eliminate unethical tobacco industry marketing practices. He is the author or coauthor of nine books on personal motivation and organizational leadership, and publisher of the *Spark Plug* newsletter, which has an international readership. Joe is a frequent speaker on values-based leadership and personal motivation, and has worked with organizations across North America to help promote a more positive and productive workplace.

Dick Schwab is a Senior Values Coach. In his previous career, he was general manager for a major division of the NCS Corporation, which he grew into $100 million business prior to overseeing it being merged with Pearson Education. In addition to his work with Values Coach, Dick is a world-class volunteer and philanthropist (including having chaired the board of Mercy Hospital in Iowa City and the national board of Scholarship America). When the Iowa City Press Citizen designated Dick as that community's "Man of the Year," it referred to him as a classic Renaissance Man. In his spare time, he crafts fine furniture which he donates to charity, and builds magnificent round stone barns that have received national recognition.

Additional Resources

You can download a poster and audio CD on *The Self-Empowerment Pledge* at **www.Pledge-Power.com** (there is no charge).

You can download the entire ebook edition of Joe's book *The Healing Tree* and companion study guide *Healing the Hospital* at **www.Healing-Story.com** (there is no charge).

The following articles special reports are available for free download at **www.JoeTye.com**:

- The Business Case for Values Training
- Moving from a Culture of Accountability to a Culture of Ownership
- 50 Great Ideas for Finding and Keeping Great People
- Leadership Lessons from the Grand Canyon
- Get that Pickle Out of Your Mouth: 9 Actions for a More Positive Attitude

Share The Florence Prescription with your Hospital Team

The Florence Prescription is ideal for:

Conference keynote and breakout sessions: Joe Tye is a dynamic, thought-provoking and inspiring speaker to kick-off or conclude your conference, and/or to provide more intensive breakout or seminar sessions.

Leadership retreats: Powerful insights for optimizing the eight essential characteristics of a culture of ownership, and for making the most of your invisible architecture of core values, corporate culture and the emotional environment of the workplace.

Caregiver retreats: Available as half-day and full-day sessions, this retreat program celebrates the proud legacy of the healing professions, places the current health care "crisis" in a proper historical perspective, and inspires confidence for a bright future.

Staff recognition events: Much more than a motivational pep rally, *The Florence Prescription* shares practical and proven strategies for personal and professional success. This high-energy program or series of presentations can energize your team to march toward an uncertain future with a spirit of confidence, pride, and fellowship.

For more information or to schedule a program
call 800-644-3889 (319-624-3889)

What hospital CEOs say

about Values Coach initiatives on
The Twelve Core Action Values

"*The Twelve Core Action Values* has been an important complement to Griffin's patient-centered philosophy of care… and has been one of the factors earning Griffin a place on *Fortune* magazine's roster of America's 100 Best Companies to Work For… But more important in my view has been the influence our commitment to *The Twelve Core Action Values* has had on individual employees. I've heard from many of our people who, as a result of this training, have made impressive personal changes."

Patrick Charmel, President and CEO, Griffin Hospital (Connecticut)

"Nothing has generated the level of excitement and energy as seen in graduates of the two-day Spark Plug training [on *The Twelve Core Action Values*]. On a personal note, this experience caused me to reflect on my own values, leading to a renewed commitment and adoption of *The Self-Empowerment Pledge*. I've personally benefited more from this interaction with Joe than from any other growth opportunity."

Fran Finley, Chief Administrative Officer, Aurora Medical Center Oshkosh (Wisconsin)

"Our initiative on *The Twelve Core Action Values* has definitely been worth the investment. The open staff sessions were extremely well attended, and had a rejuvenating effect on the entire organization. In particular, graduates of the two-day Spark Plug course are genuinely interested and engaged, and are now working together as a group helping us develop a roadmap for the cultural enhancements we wish to bring about in the years to come. This training in values-based life skills is an excellent complement to the more traditional technical subject matter that's often the focus of hospital training."

Jeff Hill, (then) President and CEO, Midwest Medical Center (Illinois)

"When we shared *The Twelve Core Action Values* with our employees and medical staff, the response was unanimous: 'We need more of this!' That's why we followed up with an intensive values initiative to train a core group of Spark Plugs to promote values-based leadership in our organization, and in our community. From Authenticity to Leadership, this is who we want to be."

Sandy Haryasz, Chief Executive Officer, Page Hospital (Arizona)

The Florence Prescription is the Gift to your People that is also an Investment in your Organization

Call the Values Coach offices for information about:

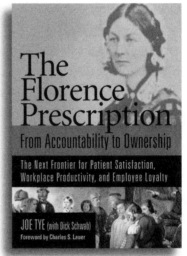

- Quantity discount schedule for *The Florence Prescription*

- Companion study guide *Putting The Florence Prescription to Work in Your Hospital, and in Your Life*

- Presentations by Joe Tye or other members of the Values Coach team

- Values Coach consulting services on cultural transformation – helping hospitals make the transition from a culture of accountability to a culture of ownership

800-644-3889 (319-624-3889)

The Healing Tree:
A Mermaid, A Poet, and A Miracle

If you enjoyed *The Florence Prescription*, you will also want to read *The Healing Tree: A Mermaid, A Poet, and A Miracle.*

www.Healing-Story.com

The Healing Story website also features the online edition of the Healing the Hospital study guide.

800-644-3889 (319-624-3889)